Published by Oldie Publications Ltd
65 Newman Street, London W1T 3EG
© 2008 The Oldie

ISBN: : 978-0954817688

Printed by MKT Print

Acknowledgements
The Oldie would like to thank all the writers, illustrators
and cartoonists whose work is reproduced in these pages.

The Oldie

ANNUAL 2009

'It's bad news I'm afraid, Mr Hall. I've been having an affair with your wife'

 **Welcome to _The Oldie_ Annual...**
With little experience of what they call 'a general interest magazine', I was advised when I helped to launch _The Oldie_ in 1992 that my job was to commission the articles which I thought it should contain. After a month or two I realised that this was a mistake. A far better approach was to allow authors to write about anything that took their fancy.

I hope that this new _Oldie_ Annual helps to make the point. Very few of the articles were commissioned and only one of the cartoons (see page 68). This gives them an originality which is not to be found in a great many other magazines.

Reading these pieces will, I hope, inspire others to try their hand.

Richard Ingrams

Olden life

What was... breach of promise?

IN P G WODEHOUSE'S *The Code of the Mulliners* a group of 'serious thinkers' is discussing how to tell a girl the engagement is off. One says: 'You get your false beard, then you write the girl a letter, then you slap on the beard and go to Nova Scotia.' Mulliner's nephew has a better idea: take her to the Savoy and have yourself loudly denounced at the table by an old flame (hired from a theatrical agency). This will put the onus of severance on the female and leave male honour intact. And there will be little risk of a suit for breach of promise.

Until a generation ago, a male breaking off an engagement faced the prospect of his supposed perfidies being splashed over the newspapers. The breach case might cost him hundreds, or only a farthing, depending on whether the jury thought the woman's tears genuine. Actions of this sort, which inspired Sir William Gilbert's *Trial By Jury* ('Comes the broken flower... Comes the cheated maid') were still being brought in the mid-20th century.

In the 1960s Marcus Lipton, MP for Brixton (recreation: giving advice), badgered ministers to abolish actions for breach, or to facilitate a Private Member's Bill with that aim. He reminded them that back in 1879 Parliament passed a resolution urging abolition. Angrily he attacked the Attorney-General's 'stick-in-the-mud' attitude: 'Will he bear in mind that this sort of action is sordid, stupid and not in line with the modern idea of sex equality? Most people want to see it abolished.' The Attorney-General (Manningham Buller) said he knew of no such demand and that it was an error to suppose that men could not sue for breach.

These 'sordid, stupid' cases enabled barristers to ask questions like: 'Do you really put yourself forward as a man of principle?' 'Are you presenting yourself to the court as a woman of virtue?' and (a deadly one, this) 'Were you not at one time an actress?' A former Miss Venus who heard herself described to the jury as 'a woman who once was beautiful' was consoled by an award of £2,000, though opposing counsel had suggested 'a very small coin'.

Much depended on whether the parties had indulged in 'intimacy' before or after becoming engaged, and how often. A woman from a harsher culture might plead that after cohabitation she could not return to her family, who would view her as damaged goods. Not seldom it turned out that the man was already married:

These 'sordid, stupid' cases enabled barristers to ask questions like (and a deadly one this): 'Were you not at one time an actress?'

one such offender, of Mediterranean origin, said he saw no reason why the plaintiff should not continue happily as his mistress. A commercial traveller who had 'mesmerised' and 'battened on' a nurse for 18 months was ordered to pay £3,289, of which £500 was for breach. 'She declared her love for me every day, week in, week out,' explained the gallant bagman. 'She gave, I accepted, and we jointly spent.' The judge said, 'Nonsense.'

An elderly woman made news by trying to sue her dead husband for breach, having found that he already had a wife when she married him, but the sympathetic judge threw out the case. One sensible couple came to a last-minute agreement, the woman saying she would keep the £850 engagement ring, but would not wear it and would probably give it to charity. Mysteriously, a representative of a cancer research fund was waiting in a court corridor, and it was handed over. In Dublin an agricultural contractor who, the judge said, had been badly treated by a woman and kept on a string for ten years was awarded a modest £144, with a settlement of other claims.

In 1969 a Law Commission recommended that an engagement to marry should no longer be an enforceable contract. The courts could make an apportionment if the parties had contracted to buy, for example, a house or a car. This recommendation was given effect in a tidying-up Act.

Since then matrimony has become a far from universal custom and the rules of courtship, so far as they exist, have been greatly relaxed. Only diehards will want to bring back the days when the young man who got cold feet went off to join the French Foreign Legion (or put on a beard and headed to Nova Scotia).

E S TURNER

'Hurry up! Hurry up! – it's that awful woman you can't stand...'

Modern life

What is...
bling-bling?

'**CHECK OUT** the bling-bling on that!' my twelve-year-old nephew Dante gasped as the Lord Mayor swished past. Dante was, of course, referring to the Lord Mayor's chain. It was big. It glittered. It was fake gold. Yes, it was genuine 24-carat bling-bling. 'Oh my days! Get me one of them things like what that old geezer's got!' Dante demanded. 'Get one for yourself,' I retorted. 'They're only £3.99 at Pound-stretcher in Harlesden.'

These days, it is not only Dante who harbours an infernal desire for bling-bling. Everyone under 21 knows that bling is the thing. Rap stars from Snoop Doggy Dogg to Li'l Bow Wow continually bark out the order, 'Get blinged or die tryin'.' Gangstas of fashion are bowed down by

> '*All them diamonds in her hair, rubies at her throat! Seems she done turned too uppity for her own safety*'

the weight of jewellery, and when the light catches the fake gems, weak eyes cry out for sunglasses. London is ablaze with bling. The necklaces swinging from the chests of today's hipsters make the Lord Mayor's look risibly puny.

Students of blingology will know it was neither Snoop Doggy Dogg nor Li'l Bow Wow who first blinged their way to glory. A hundred years ago in New Orleans, Jelly Roll Morton, the self-styled inventor of jazz, seduced the world with his diamond-studded teeth. His smile purportedly caused as great a sensation as his musical genius. His fellow-artistes, such as Bessie Smith, the Empress of the Blues, knew the wisdom of investing in spectacular bling-bling. Black audiences paid to be dazzled.

However, Bessie's flaunting extrava-gance occasionally disconcerted her white townsfolk. In 1925, the wife of La Smith's record producer lamented, 'That nigra woman! All them diamonds in her hair, rubies at her throat and a mink coat which posolutely trails on the ground! Seems she done turned too uppity for her own safety!' The Empress, in other words, was bling-blinging in an age when she should have been cringe-cringeing. Her grandmother would have worn a slave collar; sixty years later Bessie sported a diamond choker. Which brings us to the roots of bling.

Bling's source can be neatly traced to the possible ancestors of Jelly, Bessie and Snoop – the Yoruba peoples of Nigeria. No one in the world can out-bling a Yoruba. Indian saris can just about match Nigerian fabrics glitter for glitter; but the Yoruba physique is just so much beefier than anyone else's that non-Yoru-bas inevitably appear colourless in com-parison. Yorubas don't waste their nairas on poshing-up their houses, going on expensive holidays or even buying flashy electrical gadgets. They beautify them-selves. Every Yoruba man and woman is a walking work of art. Handwoven shim-mering material around the waist and cloth of gold balanced alarmingly on the head creates an effect equalled only by Chaucer's Wife of Bath, whose 'handker-chieven weighed her to the ground'.

Perhaps the most spectacular Yoruba adornments are the elaborately plaited hairstyles, which can take five whole days to complete. In a land where slavery is openly practised, it is very disconcert-ing for the dowdy foreigner to be served by a house-girl who blazes like the

'Li'l Bow Wow' all blinged up

Queen of Sheba in all her magnificence.

And now the descendants of these human pageants have colonised the world with their music and bling-bling. All over Europe, India, China, Japan, Russia – even communist Laos, style warriors are blinging it on down to the beat of Afro-America. Whatever their original language, no youngster in the world is unable to translate this phrase.

> Yo! Ho! Fo shizzle I sing,
> If you ain't got bling-bling
> You ain't got nothin' there,
> In fact, you ain't nowhere.

ZENGA LONGMORE

'Here's a February special – a five-day "Scatter His Ashes" cruise'

New York

by Patrick Cockburn

Disproportionate self-importance can make a place kinda annoying...

When I used to visit New York in the 1970s, I stayed with my brothers, Andrew and Alexander. Both had apartments in a building overlooking Central Park, and I used to look down, thinking that New York was hard to beat.

In the early 1980s, they both left New York, so the apartments on Central Park West were no longer available. Instead, I would stay in the apartment of a friend who was living with a boyfriend in Greenwich Village, which is on the other side of the park. Though when she married him, I had to start staying in hotels when I visited.

Now, I used to think that I liked New York less after that because I missed my brothers and was compelled to pay for some cramped hotel room, which always seemed, regardless of expense, to be less comfortable than hotels in other parts of the US or in Europe. But it is only in the last few years that I began to wonder if the real reason that

It is no longer the world's greatest cosmopolitan city. There is no sense of different cultures rubbing along productively together

I like New York less is that, for all its supposed glamour, it has become something of a dump.

It is not one of the great dumps of the world, mind you, but its 'dump-ishness' catches one unprepared. I used to visit Tripoli, which is a notorious dump, to interview Colonel Gaddafi – meetings that I rightly suspected were going to be cancelled at the last moment – but at least I knew before I went, so I had no sense of disappointment. I used to lie on my bed in the Libya Palace Hotel reading Jane Austen, knowing that Elizabeth Bennett's life was far more interesting than anything Tripoli had to offer.

So many things in New York are unexpectedly second-rate, you see –

hotels, restaurants, airports, public transport and taxis are all of worse quality than those in most other capitals. But, as irritating as this is, what has really put me off New York is its pretentiousness and self-importance.

To me, New York is no longer the world's greatest cosmopolitan city. There is no sense of different cultures rubbing along productively together, as in London or Miami. As a cultural centre, it is well behind the best of Western Europe. And its supreme cultural icon, *The New York Times*, played a miserable role in promoting the existence of WMD in Iraq five years ago. These days it is merely a servile conduit of dubious information from the White House and the Pentagon.

Presumably, the British visitors who have flooded into New York on cheap shopping trips have a happy time, but, walking around New York this year, I was impressed most by its mediocrity and a disagreeable sense that there were few things to do in the city that I could not do better elsewhere.

Fags for the memory

BERYL BAINBRIDGE

was told to give up the ciggies, or she might not have a leg to stand on. But kicking the habit of a lifetime has had some surprising side-effects...

On Christmas Eve last year I spent two hours in the casualty department of the Whittingham Hospital. This was due to confiding in my eldest daughter that my big toe had become frozen stiff and that I had a pain in the calf of my left leg. She, being medical, instantly thought of vascular difficulties, a diagnosis later confirmed by the doctor on duty. Days later, owing to the intervention of good friends, I was seen by a private consultant and learnt that the condition is known as claudication, from the Latin *claudicare*, meaning to limp, a distinctive style of perambulation caused by the veins in the leg, or legs, becoming blocked up. Why this should happen is mostly down to us living too long. It may also have something to do with smoking.

My father, once a consumptive boy who, at the age of ten, was employed as a cabin boy on a sailing ship to New York, was never without his pipe. During the Second World War, when tobacco was rationed, he smoked Kardomah tea leaves. Every five years or so my mother bought a packet of Craven A and transferred the contents to a silver cigarette case which was only brought out on Boxing Day. My Auntie Margo had a hacking cough and was never without a Woodbine, and my uncle, who had money, smoked very fat cigars. I had a cough too, from tuberculosis, though I never knew that until fifty years later when I underwent an X-ray for persistent bronchitis.

I became a smoker at the comparatively late age of 17 while understudying the Duchess of York in *Richard III*. The actress playing the part smoked like a chimney – though not, of course, in her Shakespearean role – and had endured a difficult love life, the details of which confused me. There was someone called

Hilary who had hit her, and a chap called George M Burton who had proposed marriage and then disappeared. 'Men,' she said, blowing smoke-rings at me, 'are to be avoided, my child. They encircle nothing but misery.'

I gave up smoking, without the aid of pills, hypnotism or patches, 17 days ago, having been told that if I didn't I mightn't have a leg to stand on. Well-meaning friends hastened to assure me that within 48 hours I would see an improvement in my complexion, my eyes, my hair. Needless to say, I'm still looking. What I have noticed, and deplore, is a return of my sense of smell. I had no idea that the odour of leftover food could pervade a house. Nor had I realised that I would regrow hairs in my nose, causing prolonged fits of sneezing.

I have no urge to take up the habit again, but I now talk to myself – mostly about Winston Churchill – sing hymns out loud while in the queue at the bank, and find it extremely difficult to construct a worthwhile sentence. I also have two recurring dreams which I remember on waking, one a rerun of that scene in the film *The Young Lions* in which Montgomery Clift lights two cigarettes, and the other of myself standing in the middle of some huge railway station listening to a voice on the loudspeaker urging me not to board the 9.45 train to Warrington.

The Churchill obsession is quite interesting. Did you know that by the time he'd turned 80 he had coronary thrombosis, three attacks of pneumonia, a hernia, two strokes and something known as a senile itch? All the same, though often setting fire to himself, he still managed to enjoy a cigar.

Whether we are in a pleasant or a painful state depends upon the kind of things that pervade and engross our consciousness. Intellectual occupations will go a long way towards one's peace of mind, always supposing one can look forward to a cigarette during or when the task is done. That I no longer can is now a serious problem, and one that seems unlikely to go away for some time, for I don't believe it has much to do with nicotine withdrawal. That's a factor, of course, but so is age and the length of time one has persisted in a habit. I simply don't feel like me without a packet of cigarettes to hand, and I have become a stranger to myself. If I was more interesting I might want to get to know me, which is an odd thought and one that swirls through my head like dissolving smoke.

ANORAK
RICHARD PERCIVAL

FOR ABOUT 25 years I've been the ridicule of my friends, my family – and of pub landlords. Why? Because I'm Britain's biggest collector of brewery advertising trays, or waiter trays, if you want to call them by their proper name. Yes, I'm talking about the tin trays on which you'd carry your drinks outside on a hot summer's day. Well, not quite, as my collection spans from the 1880s to 1970, and to have a tray still in use from the Sixties is pretty remarkable in this day and age.

When my strange hobby began, those who knew me best thought I was raving mad – especially when I gave my well-rehearsed speech to gain the attention of an unsuspecting landlord. Friends would cringe when I opened the conversation with, 'Hello, I've got an unusual hobby!'

I could see the look of horrible anticipation in the poor bar-person's face: it was almost a relief when I said I only collected beer trays. £1 in the charity box would usually do and I'd obtain a new example for my fast-growing collection. After the initial shock in the pub, my hobby became the centre-piece of conversation. Regulars in the pub would become involved, recollecting that they once had a tray advertising this old brewery or that beer.

By and large, most publicans reacted positively to my passion. However, the same cannot be said of the publican of a now-closed pub in Lancaster – one of the toughest pubs in Britain. I'd spotted a tray on the wall as I was walking past and plucked up the courage to buy a beer. I walked in with a few photos and asked for the landlord. The pub went silent. I recited my speech, as was my habit, but didn't quite get the response I expected. 'What do you want? A Blue Peter badge?' was the unfortunate answer. I was laughed out of the establishment.

With the size of my collection expanding and the number of rarer trays becoming increasingly difficult to obtain, I began to turn my attention to the media. Perhaps they could help. I'd written to the Bury Times chasing a tray from Chadwick's brewery which closed before the war. I was delighted when a gentleman phoned to say that his grandfather was Mr Chadwick, and that he had such a tray in his garage. Unfortunately, he didn't ring back, so I asked for help from the newspaper to track him down. I received a call from an historian who had been researching the Chadwick brewery for many years.

Lancashire radio had me on live with the story, and then a call came from Granada TV. In a couple of days' time, and a full three weeks of chasing this tray story, I was about to go on TV. I couldn't have guessed what was about to hit me. My girlfriend at the time took me out for a meal. She looked sheepishly at me and said: 'Don't be angry. Mr Chadwick is actually a colleague from my work. It's all been a prank.' I had been completely sucked in and couldn't believe it, though I did manage to see the funny side.

So, you thought tray collecting was dull. Today I have Britain's biggest collection, with well over a thousand trays. My collection has appeared in many magazines, been discussed on radio numerous times, and been viewed on TV twice, including on Channel 4's Collector's Lot. I'm still as passionate about the topic and I believe that I'm preserving brewery history. People are genuinely stunned when they first see my trays displayed and mickey-taking has turned to admiration.

I'm still searching for pre-war trays which can be identified by the fact that they are black coloured when you turn them over. If anyone can help a sad anorak and has a black-backed tray, I'd greatly appreciate a call on 07715 369540 – but please don't say you're a Chadwick because I won't believe you.

Watching the Wireless

by Kit Wright

Way back down in the Fifties,
Deep back dark back down in the Fifties,
When the dockers were always on strike
Except for Sir Bernard and Lady Docker
Who drove a pink Rolls Royce
And were deemed ineffable...

When, shall we say, Jack Hawkins played
The Detective Superintendent,
Said 'Wait, I've got an idea!'
And raised his trilby hat on a stick
Over the warehouse wall,
The better to draw the villain's fire
And determine his position –
HE'S OVER THERE! –
Well, round about then...

That's way back down in the Fifties,
Boom back zoom back down to the Fifties,
The family watched the wireless,
Niched like an icon in the tied
Flat with a school kitchen
Four floors down below,
And it spoke to them.
As from a ship
On the night sea with its lit and steadfast
Foreign cabin windows...
Or it hung there like a sybil
In the cave of its own sound,
And in the singing cage of the room
High in the windy trees,
They watched the wireless to see what it would say.

Miles Kington

Becoming Amabel

Long-standing, faithful Oldie contributor and friend, Miles Kington died in January 2008. This column is taken from February 1995 and is a witty tale of mistaken identity

I WENT to London and back on 10th January, the day Irritable Parker Bowles Syndrome broke out, and the evening papers were suddenly full of Camilla Divorce stories. (A Londoner might object that there is only one evening paper these days, but if you are travelling home from Paddington, you get a choice of evening papers at Reading, Bath and Bristol, and believe me they were all full of Camilla Divorce stories.)

When a story like the Camilla Divorce story breaks, you don't just get one report. You get it from all angles, especially in the *Standard*. You get Anthony Holden on the constitutional implications. You get Brian Sewell on the artistic overtones. You get photo essays on that relationship. You get a statement from the solicitor and/or the husband, including what I still think is the amazing statement that 'We have secretly been leading quite separate lives for several years' – a hard thing to do secretly, I would think. And I was reading the fourth or fifth piece on the Camilla Divorce scandal when suddenly my eyes opened wide. There, in front of me, was a picture of none other than Lady Amabel Lindsay, who apparently had once been one of Andrew Parker Bowles's old flames.

'This on-hold sitar music from Bombay is rather nice'

Who? Well, that's what I would have said, had I not once lived in Notting Hill and shared a telephone number with Lady Amabel Lindsay, or very nearly. My phone number was 6606. Hers was 6006 on the same exchange. I know that, because I often got phone calls for her.

All of Amabel Lindsay's friends who rang me seemed fairly stupid. Surely you would have to be to get a number wrong so often

'Hello, is Amabel there?' these aristocratic voices would bray. I had never heard the name Amabel till then. It sounded like a misprint for Annabel. To begin with, I would say, No. Then I got curious: so many wrong numbers for the same name...

'Amabel who?' I said one day.

'Lady Amabel Lindsay – is she there?'

She never was. After that I started asking what number they were trying to ring, and finally one of them, brighter than the rest, said it was 6006.

'Ah, but what you've dialled is 6606...'

'Is it? Oh. How do you know?'

'Because that's my number and you've just dialled me.'

'Really? I say, that's awfully clever,' this upper-class caller said. 'I say, is Amabel there?'

'No, this is 6606. The number you want is her number which is 6006. I'd try that if I were you...'

'I say, thanks most awfully.'

They never asked me how I knew her number. Perhaps they thought I was some sort of servant, or answering service. But then, all of Amabel Lindsay's friends who rang me seemed fairly stupid. Surely you would have to be a bit thick, to get such a simple number wrong so often. Whenever I answered the phone, even when giving my correct number, they always asked if Amabel

was there. That meant that a) they never listened to what they were told; b) they saw nothing odd in having Amabel's phone answered by a complete stranger.

Did that mean that Lady Amabel quite often had strange men in the house with unfamiliar voices, manning her phone? Or did it mean that her friends never suspected anything wrong until it was pointed out to them?

As time wore on and the frequency of the calls did not decrease, I started to embroider my replies.

'I say, is Amabel there?'

'No, I'm afraid the operation wasn't a success.'

'I beg your... Good Lord, what operation? What's gone wrong?'

Then I would put the phone down. Other answers I used included: 'She's helping the police with their inquiries at the moment... ' and 'Well, she's never very coherent this time of day...' and 'I'm afraid she went off with a young man last night and she isn't back yet.'

I left London and forgot all about Lady Amabel Lindsay and then suddenly there she was in the paper. It said she had been a flame of Andrew Parker Bowles, but that they had never really got it together, for some reason. I suspect I know the reason. She got cross because he never phoned. He did phone actually. Quite often. But he always got me instead.

Walking backwards in the dark while carrying a large tray of chocolates suspended by a chain from one's neck is among the most dangerous occupations known to women – and I am not forgetting wartime ambulance driving. The beginning of 1968 – year of student uprisings and the Russian invasion of Czechoslovakia – saw me treading the plush carpets of London's Theatre Royal Haymarket in a little black number and some confusion. The confusion came both from my general vagueness about money and from

Imagine a cold March Saturday night: the show over, punters chattering like birds as they filed out, a little fog creeping in

the savage nature of the theatre-going middle classes when roused. The house manager, a nice man with a wooden leg, once hissed at us as he prepared to throw open the main doors before an evening performance: 'Right, girls, hold on to your trays, here come the Cossacks!'

I had recently moved from Birmingham and was trying my luck, without much success, as a journalist down south. The Haymarket job, Wednesday and Saturday matinées and three evening performances, would be, I fondly imagined, a lifeline. 'Like the theatre, do you, dear?' asked the fat woman in the box-office. 'Oh, yes,' I said. Well I did. I'd taken part in an ATS training camp Christmas revue and once interviewed a lion at Bertram Mills

Haunted house

After an unfortunate incident in the Stalls at the Theatre Royal, novice choc-ice seller **PAULA KELLY** *was banished to the Gods, where she had a strange encounter...*

Circus. I was not, however, prepared for the rigours of the auditorium. It was in the Stalls that I began my short-lived theatrical career.

The play was a starry revival of *The Importance of Being Earnest*, with Isabel Jeans as Lady Bracknell, Daniel Massey as Jack, John Standing as Algernon, Celia Bannerman as Cicely, Helen Weir as Gwendolyn, Robert Eddison as Canon Chasuble and the splendid Flora Robson as Miss Prism. On Wednesday 7th February 1968 there was to be a Gala Preview in the presence of the Queen Mum, and the trays were shaking. 'It'll be all right, Polly' (he

never could get my name right), said the house manager. 'Her Nibs won't come down here, and even if she does it'll be gin an' whatsit she'll be after.' Suitably calmed, I watched everything go to plan: packed house, the Nat Ant, the QM waving nicely, and the first act purring along. Lady B came and went, the 'handbag' line managed to survive Edith Evans, and when the curtain fell on John Standing, alone on the stage, smirking at his shirt-cuff, there was thunderous applause. It was the interval that was my undoing.

The queue went fine, and I even managed to give everybody their cor-

'Well, this explains why the cruise was so cheap!'

'Worry lines – I like to see that in an employee'

rect change. The third interval bell had rung and people were back in their seats when a large man in Row B beckoned. I advanced. 'Choc-ice!' he barked. I smiled and, reaching forward to hand it to him, caught the right-hand loop of my tray chain in the hair of the woman next to him. She shrieked, I fell and a shower of choc-ices and assorted confectionery shot across bosom and knee and rolled gently beneath the reinforced undersides of seats. At this point the lights went down, and the sound of summer birdsong that opened Act II was pungently mixed with the cries of gentry in distress. The house manager was very nice about it afterwards, but the theatre received a fairly hefty cleaning bill and I went home early.

Actually, I wasn't sacked but banished to the Circle, where I was personally responsible for stopping the practice of serving hot tea to patrons in their seats, and thence – apotheosis – to the Gods. Here I was much more comfortable. A nicer class of person, you might say, and far more tolerant of rogue tray-ladies. I might have served my time very happily up there but for the Ides of March and the incident with another Mr B.

Imagine a cold March Saturday night: the show over, punters chattering like birds as they filed down the stairs to the street and me doing what we used to call the 'mop-up', checking for discarded jewellery, usable cash and broken glass. A little fog had crept in from outside and was floating through the exit door as I moved methodically along the rows. Getting towards the back I turned and saw a man standing at the end of the front row, looking down into the body of the theatre. 'Can I help you?' I asked in my best Theatre Royal tones. No response. 'Have you lost something?'

'Can I help you?' I asked in my best Theatre Royal tones. 'Have you lost something?' The figure turned and looked at me

The figure turned and looked at me.

A stoutish man with rather wild hair and a crumply face – W C Fields meets Gordon Brown – left elbow bent and left hand resting lightly on the lapel of his long, dark coat. Still saying nothing, he began to climb the stairs towards me.

He wore a tan double-breasted waistcoat, rather old-fashioned, baggy trousers, large bow tie and carried in his right hand a black top hat with silk lining. As he passed me, he mouthed something and, turning left, walked to the exit and disappeared. I went after him a little way but could see nothing down the misty stone staircase that led to the street.

The house manager was standing in the foyer. 'Everything under control, Polly?' 'I think so,' I said. Then I told him about the figure in the Gods. 'Ah,' said the HM. 'Fancy a drink, Poll?'

We had one in the pub round the corner, shandy for him, Bloody Mary for me. Pulling a crumpled photo out of his pocket, he passed it over without a word. It was the man I'd seen, right down or up to the top hat. What's more, it had the look of a daguerreotype or engraving, not a proper photo. 'Name of Buckstone,' said the HM. 'John Baldwin Buckstone, known as Bucky, manager of the Theatre Royal from 1853. You should have caught his Aguecheek. Hangs around a lot, does Bucky, though it's not everyone sees him. Only a matter of time before you did, though, Poll. You're the type.'

I think I had two more Bloody Marys before HM saw me to the Tube. And I worked out the rest of my term in the Ladies' Cloakroom. On the whole I preferred coats to ghosts, even when they're worn by large women from Wapping. But that's another story.

'Would you like me to throw that in the river for you, sir?'

Dr Haire, far left, and his colleagues at the Geneva Sex Congress

Congress interruptus...

Dr Norman Haire told **STANLEY PRICE** *rather more than he wished to know about sex*

Before sex education, before Kinsey, Comfort and the many loves that finally dared to speak their names, most of us somehow managed to find out what constituted the best part of a private life. Our education usually came by word of mouth, mainly from our peers. There were also books that got passed around. In my time the most popular were Dr Eustace Chesser's *Love Without Fear* and any of the works of Dr Norman Haire that you could lay your hands on. I remember being astounded by some of the things included in his *Encyclopedia of Sexual Practice*, even though I never got beyond 'H' before it was snatched away from me. I was particularly astonished that on the title page his credit was 'by Dr Norman Haire, President of the Sex Congress of Geneva'. My mind boggled at what went on at a Sex Congress, let alone in Geneva.

By the time I was called up for National Service, I reckoned I was suf-

ficiently knowledgable in sexual matters. The problem was finding the opportunity to apply one's knowledge. Despite all the foul language, filthy limericks and vile songs of my fellow National Servicemen, I reckon there was a more than fifty per cent virginity rate. However, halfway through National Service, I had an unforgettable sexual experience. My oldest friend Wally and I were on leave in London at the same time. It was a Thursday night and we were looking for some affordable entertainment. I had bought a *New Statesman*, and going down the events columns a name leapt out at me – Dr Norman Haire. That evening at the Conway Hall, Red Lion Square, Holborn, he was addressing the Rationalist Society of Great Britain on 'The Rationalist Approach to Sex'. No question where we were going.

Since the 1930s the Conway Hall had been the meeting-place for a wide range of radical groups, from pacifist socialists

through vegans and naturists to theosophists and the followers of Gurdjieff and Blavatsky. The audience that night looked like a cross-section of all of them. I suspected that some of the women in flowing smocks and dirndl skirts were

'And have my boys washed their hands?'

naturists on a night out. A lot of men were wearing tweed suits that looked homemade, worn with boots or sandals. Most surprisingly dressed of all, when he appeared, was Dr Norman Haire himself. He was wearing a baggy, bright purple corduroy suit. He was in his fifties, fat and had a large walrus moustache. Not exactly a figure one would associate with sex, rational or otherwise.

After a fulsome introduction by the chairman, Dr Haire was on his feet. His voice was loud and rather harsh. It is now half-a-century ago, but his opening lines are engraved indelibly on my memory. 'I am sorry but tonight I am going to shock you. So let's start with the worst first – necrophilia, sleeping with a dead body.'

There was such a massive intake of communal breath that it was as though all the oxygen had been sucked out of the room. I glanced at Wally. His jaw had dropped. 'You sleep with a dead body. You're put on trial. If you're found guilty you're given a ten- or twelve-year sentence. But whom have you hurt? Nobody. Rape a young woman, bring an unwanted life into the world and what happens? The victim is humiliated in court and argued over. And, if found guilty, what does the man get? Three, maybe four years in jail. Is that rational? No. Nothing about our sex laws is rational.'

He launched into a free-ranging tirade against any kind of sexual repression. His technique was to proceed by a series of shocking and angry questions. 'Masturbation!' he shouted. 'Why is it called self-abuse? Why "abuse"? Nobody goes blind. Take it from me, it doesn't stunt growth. Why the word "abuse", then? To create guilt, that's why! Like everything else in our society concerned with sex.'

I sneaked a look round. Wally had managed to get his jaws back together, but his eyes looked very poppy. The rest of the audience remained frozen, aghast, clearly dreading the next awful perversion the President of the Sex Congress of Geneva would hurl at them. Of course, today nothing much he said would have unduly disturbed an average post-watershed TV viewer. But that evening in the Conway Hall, even for the most free-loving, vegetarian Trot, Dr Norman Haire was light-years ahead of his time. For a full fifty minutes he spared his audience nothing. No chink or kink of sexual behaviour escaped his attention. As he built to a climax on consenting sado-masochism, sweating profusely, walrus moustache glistening, arms

outstretched, he became for a moment a religious figure – a Messiah in purple corduroy.

He sat down to a stunned silence. Then British politeness overcame shock and there was some awkward applause. The chairman asked for questions. After a long embarrassing pause a few hands went up in the air. Several halting, innocuous questions were asked. The audience began to unfreeze. As people

He built to a climax on consenting sado-masochism, sweating profusely, walrus moustache glistening, arms outstretched

whispered to their neighbours there was a sort of background twittering. Hands were shooting up on all sides. In the row in front of us a small, middle-aged man had been waving his arm, trying desperately to attract the chairman's eye. Finally the chairman acknowledged him. The man got up nervously. 'Dr Haire, you mentioned several forms of birth control. There was one I think you didn't mention. Would you like to say something about ... er ... other forms?'

'What other forms?' Dr Haire's tone was aggressive. 'What is it?' The man mopped his brow with a handkerchief, voice just audible. 'I'd rather not say – not in mixed company.'

Dr Haire was incredulous. 'Not in mixed company – when we've already talked about necrophilia, coprophilia, incest, sodomy, bestiality. Come on, what is it?' The man mopped more and looked close to a heart attack. 'I'd rather not say.'

Dr Haire leaned towards the man. 'What is it, then? Condom – French letter? Dutch cap?' The man shook

his head. 'Douche? Ordinary pessary? Foaming pessary?' The man kept shaking his head and mopping his brow. Dr Haire lowered his voice and spoke very slowly. 'Is it coitus interruptus – withdrawal?'

'Yes,' the man gasped. Dr Haire flew into an extraordinary rage. He pointed at the man, addressing the whole audience. 'For years this man has pestered me with letters and telegrams advocating this vile, disgusting method of birth control that demeans the very nature of the sexual act. It is foul and repugnant and not even very effective. Get him out of here. I will not talk while that man is in the hall.'

In a total silence Dr Haire sat down and folded his arms. His questioner, looking as though he was having the heart attack, sat down. Then two large, younger men appeared beside him and whispered something to him. Did the Rationalist Society of Great Britain have bouncers? The man was escorted from the hall. It was too much for Wally and me. We were both writhing with suppressed laughter. My ribs ached. My eyes were watering. We nodded at each other, got up and just made it out of the hall. Sitting on a bench there, his head in his hands, was the coitus interruptus advocate. Out in the street we doubled up, howling with post-traumatic laughter.

We were still laughing uncontrollably when we went into a pub a hundred yards up the street. It was hard to get our order out to the barman. 'Seen a funny film, have you?' he said.

I took a firm grip of myself. 'No. It was better than a film – much better.'

'How about sharing the joke, then?'

'Ever heard of Dr Norman Haire?' Wally said. The barman shook his head. 'Next time you see he's talking somewhere you've got to catch him.'

'What's he talk about?'

We couldn't tell him. The hysterics had returned.

JUNE AND GERALD by NAF

An **Object** for a Walk

FRANCIS KING
abandons decision-making in favour of serendipity and the London bus network

At a session with my doctor, he asked me, with amazing optimism, 'Do you play any sports?' I replied 'No, not for at least fifty years – and then only ping-pong.' 'In that case you must walk for at least half-an-hour every day.' His was the parental severity that the young so often show to the ancient.

After that I began daily to rack my brains to find an object for a walk. But the search taxed my ingenuity. A trek with some shoes with worn-down heels to the cheap Moroccan cobbler near Ladbroke Grove rather than to the expensive one in Kensington High Street? Yet another look at the Diana Ditch in Hyde Park, with which I have been morbidly obsessed ever since, two days after its opening, I slithered in the morass then surrounding it, eventually to be hauled to my feet by a giggling young Italian couple?

Then a few months ago, I devised another strategy. Instead of struggling to find the object for a walk, I should let the walk find the object. This is how it goes. I walk to my nearest bus stop and take whatever bus comes first. As soon as something attracts my notice – a farmers' market, a crowd assembled around a fleet of police cars – I get off to make an inspection. Having done that, I clamber aboard the next bus. So it con-

tinues, with my frequently being carried into areas of London totally unfamiliar to me, until a glance at my watch or, in winter, the premature fading of the light, prompts me take a bus that I am certain is headed back home.

One of my most fruitful recent itineraries went as follows. I began with a crowded 27 bus. Before we arrived at Turnham Green, I caught sight of what had once been a cavernous fleapit to which, during the War years, my youthful sisters and I would often re-

treat from austerity and boredom. It is now an antique supermarket. Happily I wandered, gazing at things that I neither needed nor wanted. Some heavily embroidered linen sheets caught my eye. A large woman in a tent-like coat paused, eyed me and then advised: 'It's wiser to go for polyester these days. Real sheets have to be laundered and that costs a bomb.' Majestically she sailed on. Clearly – and rightly – she had surmised that a bomb was something that I could now ill afford.

The next bus, an empty 391, took me to Kew Bridge, where, on an impulse, I walked down the tow path to Zoffany House, the home of the famous painter of that name and, some two centuries later, of a less famous painter who signed her work 'E. Box'. I stood in front of her enchanting house and gazed up at it. My final visit there, shortly before her death, had been for Christmas lunch, with a mutual friend as the only other guest. After we had seated ourselves in the chilly dining-room, a wan, elegantly dressed French *au pair* brought in our food, impeccably cooked. She was introduced and, having not been invited to join us, retreated to the kitchen. Suddenly our hostess cried out 'Louise! Bread sauce! Bread sauce!' I got to my feet. 'Let me get it.' The poor girl, who had either not heard the summons or had decided to ignore it, was seated in the tiny, dingy kitchen, list-

I racked my brains to find an object for a walk, but the search taxed my ingenuity

lessly sawing at a slice of turkey. Although I had always thought that, like Chekhov's Ranevskaya, E. Box was pathetically marooned in a property far beyond her means, she left several millions. Now, gazing at the house, I felt a brief stab of grief for the loss of her vivacious company. Then I thought: always so kind and considerate to me, how could she have been so cruel to that lonely French girl, on Christmas Day of all occasions?

My final bus was a 65 to Kew Gardens, where I wandered among the magnificent Henry Moore sculptures looming through a now gathering mist. Since it was a Monday and the weather was uninviting, there were mercifully few people around. Eventually I came across a young couple, perched high up on one of the sculptures and sharing a cigarette to inhale what I guessed was not nicotine. Busybody that I have become in old age, I shouted up: 'You oughtn't to be sitting up there. Can't you read the notices? No touching, no climbing.'

'Oh, f*** off you, you silly old git.' It was the girl who responded, in a posh, bored, disdainful voice.

I at once f***ed off – this time to take not another bus, but a reviving cup of tea and an éclair in the Maids of Honour, followed by a train home. I felt satisfied. Once again the silly old git's bus lottery had come up trumps.

An Orthodox Voice
An evening of stand-up non-comedy

CIRCUMSTANCES too elaborate to detail caused me to be in a room over a pub, watching an entertainment by 'stand-up comics'. I soon wished I was elsewhere, but you could not get out of the place without upsetting the stand-ups.

It was a pathetic show and even the performers knew it. Some of them apologised for their inadequacies and appealed for sympathy. Others were angry and menacing, and one or two were literally mad. A poor youth stood up to begin his act and was suddenly possessed by a demon. Incoherent speech, peppered with filth and blasphemy, poured out of him, while the audience giggled uneasily. None of the stand-ups displayed any wit or said anything that was even meant to be funny. They mimed and pulled faces to tapes of ugly music or imitated someone on a TV show.

When it was all over and you were allowed a drink, I learnt that these stand-ups were not just self-indulgent. They were good people, and wanted to help others less fortunate than themselves. Some of them were teachers of stand-up comedy. They held courses, mainly for disadvantaged youths, the idea being that by encouraging them to stand up and shout out whatever came into their minds, they were fostering their 'self-expression'.

Oh dear, I thought, as I often do. These good people are totally misled, as they often are. What they are doing is exposing their vulnerable pupils to demonic obsession. Free-flow babble is demonically flavoured, and the more you practise it the more nasty it becomes. What they should be doing is getting them to sing in choirs.

Disturbed souls need harmony, and harmony means music. Modern psychiatry does not acknowledge that, but in traditional therapy music was the most effective art in the healing of disordered minds. Nowadays we hardly ever sing together, so there is no real harmony between us, but I remember years ago the singing in churches and chapels, in pubs and social gatherings. We do not sing any more, because someone on television does it for us.

Plato put it bluntly. If you want a harmonious society you have to sing together. And when you sing, you dance. He recommended three types of choir for three different age groups, with the same mode of music but in different tempos. For young people it was a lively chorus with amusing lyrics. For the respectably married and middle-aged it was high-minded and romantic. The third chorus was for old people. They were not required to dance, but repeated to each other their time-honoured stories and folk wisdom. That is what I do these days, with elderly cronies at parties.

The stand-ups do not approve of choirs,

> *Nowadays we hardly ever sing together, so there is no real harmony between us*

because they associate them with indoctrination. But when I was a youth doing National Service, one of our pleasures was marching to the music of the band. I turned on Channel 4 the other day and heard about the young people in China, how they too have to march to a military band. The BBC lady was disapproving of this. She interviewed some Chinese girls and invited their disapproval. But they all said they enjoyed marching to the band and did not think they were disadvantaged by lack of drugs, fashion and junk food. The marching and music brought order into their lives.

Yes, I know. Every fascistic or communist regime makes people march to their approved music. Music is the most influential of the arts. It can be used for nationalistic purposes and for whoremongering. But it can also be used for attuning souls to the harmonies that are innate in them. That is why Plato wanted us to sing together. If you have a child, the best favour you can do it is to expose it to good music. And if it goes a bit dotty, try to dissuade it from becoming a stand-up comedian.

JOHN MICHELL

VOICES FROM THE GRAVE

Every month, Oldie readers send in extracts and quotes from long-ago published books which still have a quite uncanny relevance today...

'If I were Director of Programmes for the BBC (and I shall be looking for a job after the war), I think I should admit that a 17-hour day is too long to be filled with first- or even second-rate material; and I should ration the good stuff at my disposal and stay off the air for the rest of the time, instead of trying to eke it out with trash. Better to preserve an hour's silence, better (if you must have a noise) to hand over to the BBC signal, rather than spread alarm and despondency by giving a free rein to the entertainment world.'
Taken from Nicholas Monsarrat's 'H M Corvette', from his *Three Corvettes* collection, first published in 1943

'Saturday 23rd October, 1954: To Bristol for a recording of a programme for the younger generation (15–25-year-olds). What emerged was
1. Great ignorance about Parliament and its work.
2. Cynicism about politicians and their sincerity.
3. Great gap between politicians and young people.
4. No inspiration of young people by politicians.
5. Healthy disregard of politicians' conceit.
6. Dislike of Party or intra-Party squabbles except as entertainment.'
Spotted in Tony Benn's *Diaries*

'Feb 17, 1926: Modern young women are turning to drink and drugs in a desperate bid to cope with their hectic lives, a doctor warned today. Dr J S Russell told the Institute of Hygiene that an abnormal lifestyle of nights of frivolity, followed by days of excitement, coupled with the poisons of tobacco and alcohol, strained the nervous system. "Scarcely has the age of 20 been reached before the lines that belong to the face of a woman of middle age have become evident in such girls." His words follow a warning from another eminent doctor, who condemned the current craze for the willowy figure. Such women, in trying to look like "weak and weedy men", could increase the risk of consumption.'
From *The Chronicle of the Twentieth Century*

'It is observed that a corrupt society has many laws. I know not whether it is not equally true that an ignorant age has many books. When the treasures of ancient knowledge lie unexamined, compilers and plagiarists are encouraged to give us again what we had before, and grow great by setting before us what our own sloth had hidden from our view.'
Samuel Johnson, quoted in an issue of *The Rambler*.

'The mischiefs that have arisen to the public from inconsiderate alterations in our laws are too obvious to be called into question ... The common law of England has fared like other venerable edifices of antiquity, which rash and inexperienced workmen have ventured to new-dress and refine, with all the rage of modern improvement. Hence frequently its symmetry has been destroyed, its proportions distorted, and its majestic simplicity exchanged for specious embellishments and fantastic novelties.'
From Sir William Blackstone's *Commentaries on the Laws of England*, 1765

'Since the majority of newspapers print pure lies and they lie thoroughly, then it is clever of them to clean their posteriors with these papers. There is no better use for them. They believe that with these papers the faeces is cleaned from their rears, but this is neither clear nor obvious. It is not clear whether in reality their rears are cleaned by the papers, or whether the newsprint is purified by the excrement.'
Mizra Fattah on the English, from *Shab Nameh*, published in 1842

GRANNY ANNEXE

Virginia Ironside

Dear guests – please keep your shoes on and don't even think about arriving early...

I recently had a dinner party. I know they're completely out of date, and the line-up on the table of different glasses, and rows of cutlery reaching into infinity like one of those Amaze Your Eyes trick pictures is always guaranteed to put me in a mood – yet one in four can still be tremendous fun.

Only three things drove me nuts. One was that one of the guests arrived early. Just two minutes early – but it's amazing what I plan to do in the two minutes before the guests arrive. Have a bath, dry my hair, put on my make-up, turn on the potatoes – and if someone arrives so much as two minutes early when I've still got my towel wrapped around me, it puts me out no end. By the time I've settled them with a drink, the other guests have appeared,

and before I know where I am, I'm having to play hostess in my dressing-gown and serve up raw potatoes.

The next guest took his shoes off at the door. What kind of weird behaviour is that? New etiquette? What did he think my carpet was for? Or my hoover? I'm afraid I rather tartly asked him to put them back on again, because I didn't want his smelly, socky feet seeping sweat into my carpet.

All went well until, after supper, a guest asked if he could smoke in the garden. 'Certainly not,' I said crossly. 'I don't want you luring some other amusing person outside to have an entertaining conversation leaving us miserable non-smokers to rot inside. You are only allowed to smoke in the house. Indeed, you are encouraged to smoke in

'You are only allowed to smoke in the house. Indeed, you are encouraged to smoke in the house'

the house. Why do you think there is a proliferation of ashtrays on this table?'

Put like that I don't expect any of you will ever come to dinner if I ask you. But at least my parties have a far higher success rate than the theatre.

After my major operation last year and before my major operations this year (I've decided to get rid of the bag and have a reversal) I'm left with what I think is called a snagging list. It's a phrase more usually used after the builders have left the house – when there are loose wires to be fixed and the odd bit of plastering to finish. But although I've sorted out the worst of the list – splitting wounds, dreadful scare after eating beetroot when I thought I was poo-ing blood, and so on, the nastiest is the fact that, as a result of taking so many steroids, my adrenal glands have atrophied. (I visualise them as a couple of shrivelled brown things, similar to the kind of objects found in a Pharaoh's tomb, which archaeologists puzzle over for decades.)

What happens when you take steroids

is that they say to your adrenal glands (who usually produce the cortisol provided by the steroids): 'There, there, little chappies, we're here now, you needn't do any more work. Just go to sleep.' The idea is that when you get off steroids the adrenals wake up and take over again. But mine are like dreadful teenagers. However much you shout, they won't wake up. Occasionally one grunts, and yells: 'ALL RIGHT I'M GETTING UP! STOP SHOUTING!' – but after that, nothing. There is hope, however. The endocrinologist has assured me that he's discovered a sign of life – perhaps he spotted them coming down in the middle of the night and stealing things from the fridge.

My fancy pigeon is still with me. The eminent Rupert Sheldrake (of morphic resonance fame) assures me that in the spring he will find a mate, and will either flee to the woods with her and produce a lot of boring, quiffless, pigeon babies or, more likely, lure her to his sumptuous pad at my house, where he gets fed every day. I rang a Fancy Pigeon Society and asked if he might be lonely. 'Lonely? Not likely!' replied a cockney voice. 'Why would 'e need a friend when 'e's already got one?' 'But he hasn't got a friend, that's the problem,' I replied, tearfully. 'Oh yes 'e 'as,' she replied. 'It's yew!'

I suppose when no one comes to dinner any more because I'm so bad-tempered, I can join my pigeon for a nice meal of corn on the windowsill. He's certainly better company than a lot of people I sit next to at supper.

Sunset Strip

What shall I do now that I've finished writing a biography, pondered **SARA WHEELER**. *I know! I'll take my clothes off …*

I recently published a biography. Emerging from that foetid life-writing tunnel in which I had spent three years bent over a desk in provincial archives alone with a long-dead subject, I found myself casting round for a new interest that brought me into contact with real live human beings. How treacherously easy it had been to lead someone else's life instead of my own! Action was required. The acquisition of a new skill, perhaps, at one of the multitudinous night school courses on offer in the capital. I toyed with origami, yoga, Irish-dancing for beginners and car maintenance before hitting on the ideal hobby for the jaded biographer. I enrolled at the London School of Striptease.

This august but little-known institution offers a range of workshops and courses with names like 'Grin and Bare It'. After a series of helpful conversations with the owner and sole instructor, Jo King, I opted for a two-hour one-to-one starter session. The school does not have a permanent home, but rents space in various halls, so I met Jo on a rainy night in an exciting cloak-and-dagger operation involving co-ordinated mobile phone calls and a café in St John's Wood.

Jo drove me to the hall in her Mini. She is a voluptuous, salt-of-the-earth character in her early forties, with aspirin-white English skin and Pre-Raphaelite hair the colour of butter. She has been stripping for more than twenty years, returning to the profession after a spell abroad when she had to raise cash

Jo King reveals all

'Think of yourself as a gift, unwrapping yourself slowly with delight at each new part that you reveal'

in order to get her cat out of quarantine. The small late-Victorian brick hall she had rented for the night smelled of Jeyes cleaning fluid; it had a blocked-up fireplace and, round the sides, Formica tables strewn with sheets of paper recording the minutes of a Neighbourhood Watch committee meeting. Mysteriously, a tin of Pedigree Chum stood on the mantelpiece.

Jo studied my attire and picked an outfit for herself from a voluminous portable wardrobe of lace, net, nylon and feathers. Before the off (so to speak), we perched on a couch under the Arctic light of a fluorescent tube while Jo zipped through the ground rules. Cut labels out of underwear, as they tend to stick out; always wear stockings and high heels; never wear a dress or top that goes over the head. 'And remember,' she added as she stood up to insert a *Best of the Eagles* cassette in the tape player she had brought, 'to peel off any errant bits of lavatory paper that might be clinging to your fanny.'

The basics were obvious enough, once you knew them: use all the space available, give the punters a good look at each new bit as it is revealed, throw lascivious glances over your shoulder and, above all, make eye contact. Actually getting my clothes off with a degree of seductive elegance was trickier than anticipated.

'Think of yourself as a gift, unwrapping yourself slowly with delight at each new part that you reveal,' Jo told me. She demonstrated undoing her bra with her back to the audience, swivelling round with her hands crossed across her chest, then lowering both straps simultaneously with her fingers while keeping the bra pinned to the sides of her body with her upper arms while bending forward. To me this was a baffling Houdini-like manoeuvre, and it was at this point, catching a glimpse of myself in the mirror as the Eagles worked their relentless way through 'Hotel California', that I realised the enormity of my Marks & Spencer's pants.

We struggled on, twisting and shimmying and flicking. Jo explained the dynamics of hip-wriggling and adviced against lighting the venue with candles on health and safety grounds. There was a lot of bending involved; the mantelpiece turned out to be an essential prop for what Jo called 'bottom work'. I found myself reading the Pedigree Chum label.

In the church next door, a team of bell-ringers began practising. Above their tuneful peels I heard Jo say that it was important to fling all garments well clear as they were discarded, otherwise the floor swiftly resembled an obstacle course. Also, it was vital to bring the legs together before embarking on the removal of the lower garments. I failed to grasp the mechanics of this operation, and repeatedly fell over while grappling with my knickers.

Jo is a born teacher. Articulate and methodical, she thought carefully about the best way of explaining each move, and took the trouble to offer praise and encouragement even when it was painfully clear that none was due. She is the real thing, an old pro and a showgirl of the Shirley Bassey school of entertainment. I liked her enormously, and when I had completed my first solo routine and stood flushed before her wearing only my stockings as the Eagles droned tinnily to a halt, she clapped her hands and gave me a big bare-bosomed hug.

While we were dressing she talked enthusiastically about the business plan she had devised. Having traded for two years with no advertising and proved that demand for her service exists, she now intends to market the school more aggressively. Although she is happy to offer advice about job opportunities, her core market does not consist of putative professionals. 'Only about five per

There was a lot of bending. The mantelpiece turned out to be an essential prop for what Jo called 'bottom work'

cent of my clients are looking for work. The rest want to strip for fun – many of them not even for a specific man.' Her oldest student so far has been 56. 'I'm

longing to teach an 80-year-old,' she said. 'Seduction is in the mind.'

Despite her optimistic prognosis for the school, it turns out that stripping, like everything else, has changed for the worse. 'In the old days a girl had 25 minutes,' she opined, her eyes shining as she recalled a Homeric age of poky clubs cloudy with the smoke of un-tipped Players. 'We used elaborate props – I had a friend who took half a carload down to Soho twice a week. Now you get three minutes if you're lucky.' The bell-ringers reached a crescendo, Jo pushed her long, buttery hair behind her ears and smiled wanly, the Freddie Trueman, now, of the feather boa. 'It's all about money these days.'

Despite my gargantuan underwear and outsize lack of ability, Jo made me feel that enjoying myself was all that matters. I have not performed since. (I rushed home after the class to demonstrate my new skills to my husband, but he had fallen asleep listening to *Gardener's Question Time*.) Nor have I yet informed the Society of Authors so that other spent biographers can refresh their appetites. But I often think about stripping, and now, returned to the provincial archives, I catch myself spinning fantasies of undressed victory over the cold and closely buttoned dead.

• *Contact the London School of Striptease on 07958 314 107. Website: www.lsos.co.uk*

'Oh, and your ex-wife called'

That sinking feeling...

Trapped with her two children in quicksand, Mary Cecil Pook caught a strange look in her husband's eyes — he couldn't really be thinking of walking away, could he?

It was the only summer holiday we had as a family. The acceptance of my novel for publication had unsettled my husband, perhaps to the degree of needing to restore his self-esteem. The same day that, puzzled, I consulted the kitchen calendar and realised that I must be pregnant was also the day I realised he was serious about a woman he worked with.

However, I was confident that the week away would make everything come right. Admittedly, it had been a mistake opening my own bank account in my pen-name without telling him (he would have stopped me, that's for sure), but I so longed to surprise him with a dressing-gown for his birthday. We didn't have a joint account and I had to save out of the housekeeping money for presents. Any money I was given by relatives at

Christmas or on birthdays was whisked away – of course, orchestral musicians were abysmally paid at this time, 1959, so I understood the necessity – for the quarterly bills and so forth.

We had two planned children already, one of each kind. Left to arrange details for the holiday, I chose the most reasonable lodgings at the nearest coastal resort, a tiny place I'd never heard of. The landlady was round and pleasant, we were her only self-catering guests and it was a nice house with a small garden. But the nearby beach was a disappointment – sandy enough but huge, with the sea a long way off. The children got tired just walking to it, though they forgot when actually in the water. An empty silent expanse, we were always the only people on the beach.

The worst part was after the bathe,

faced with the long trudge back. On this particular day, our little boy started grizzling and asking to be carried. My husband, preoccupied with his thoughts, was irritated and strode on ahead. I picked up the child, then the little girl was jealous and dragged on my hand so I was virtually pulling her weight along.

Suddenly, from firm footing we stepped into soft, yielding sand. It was an effort to lift one foot, then move the other up. Now both children were wailing. We were sinking down into the sand, every step more of a struggle until ... we were standing still, unable to move forward.

Calling out to my husband, my stomach became a black hollow. When a child, I had been horrified by a story about a pony named Heather who sank in a quicksand while her best horse friend looked on helplessly. They said goodbye to each other. The end was described in graphic lingering detail.

Suddenly, from firm footing we stepped into soft, yielding sand. Now both children were wailing ...

All the feelings which had traumatised me then were now engulfing and gripping me like a claw.

My husband turned and stood watching us. Away in his deeply-in-love dream world, he was seeing this miracle happening before his eyes: the ground opening to swallow the obstacle of us. Equally unbelieving, we watched him watching us.

One minute there was nobody on the beach. The next, as if from nowhere a man came swiftly running. He reached us, pulled us on to firm sand, then led us back to my husband – who was laughing it off as if only joking. But the man ignored him, walked away without a word or smile, and I was too shaken to thank him. There was no sign of him when we continued back to the house, the children reassured and comforted.

While I was putting them to bed that evening, my husband slipped away and had a long conversation with Mrs Pearce, our landlady – well, more of a monologue really, as the murmur I could hear was mainly his voice. Back upstairs he gave me a strange look, a sort of satisfied small smile behind it, but not as half as strange as Mrs Pearce's expression at breakfast next morning. For the rest of

the week she avoided speaking to me, and all the pleasantness was snuffed out. I guessed my husband had told her some tale or other just in case, getting his version in first. He needn't have bothered: my early conditioning inhibited any such disloyalty.

It was all so indigestible. I persuaded myself I'd been mistaken: the Heather story had caused me to panic and I was imagining things. I never told anyone until long after my divorce the following year, when there was a second daughter, born on St Valentine's Day, would you

'Cats are so mysterious, aren't they? You never quite know what they're thinking'

believe. There was a woman with whom I felt a rapport. It was at a house-party holiday for one-parent families, and we were unlikely to meet again. Sitting together on another beach, she listened in silence, then after a longish pause said she'd had a similar experience, standing at the end of a pier with her disenchanted husband. She had become aware – intuitively or telepathically – that he wanted to throw her over the rail into the sea. She had turned and walked quickly back to the shore, saying it was getting a bit chilly.

In both cases an unforeseen opportunity had presented itself, provoking an overwhelming temptation. There is a great difference between such an impulse and a planned murder, we agreed. All the same, we stared at one another uncomfortably. We had survived. How many others hadn't?

In my eighties now, the vivid memory still erupts occasionally, pounding on my mind as if it was only yesterday. Then I have to rub it out all over again. I've often wondered about our rescuer and wish I'd made some attempt to find him and say thank you. Then again, as he'd vanished as mysteriously as he had appeared, was he a man at all? Or was it an angel assuming human form for a matter of minutes? You do hear about such things.

Our Betty

MAVIS NICHOLSON *talks to actor and writer* **LIZ SMITH** *about the emotional legacy of rejection and her newly found happiness in a retirement home*

I went to meet Liz Smith at her new flat in a retirement home in North London. She nearly knocked me off my feet when she told me on the phone that she felt so happy and liberated there. Am I hearing right? What? Happy and liberated in an old people's home?

The warden greeted me, and when she knew I was seeing Liz she exclaimed that her arrival had cheered up the place no end. Brought new life to it. Taken years off the place.

When I told Liz this she said that it was they who had given new life to her. She was the one brightened up by the companionship when she wanted some. But at the same time, there was respect for one's privacy. This was freedom, as the responsibility of running a three-storey house had been too much for her. 'You see, if there is one word that sums up the theme of my life,' Liz said, 'it is loneliness. Right from being a child. From the death of my mother when I was two.' Could you remember her, I interjected? 'No. But she haunts my life – she's always with me. I know we had a marvellous time together because everyone said so. Yes, lonely is the word I'd use. I've lived in houses all the time and you are never sure of neighbours, you never know whether they are going to say good morning. So when you go out to a job you come back to an empty house. But, here you have people around, and they are always nice.

'I lived with my grandma and my granddad after my mother died because my father just cleared off. I never saw him again. It leaves a desolation that never leaves you. He was a very young, mad man my father. Throwing you up into the sky. Buying you jewels and sweeties. Mad, mad but I adored him, of course. I can still hear my Dad saying "I'll see you, kid. I'll write to you, kid", and waving until he was out of sight. I never saw him again. For five years I stood, after school, in the bay window in our living-room beside a big wind-up gramophone waiting for him to come back or write. He never ever did. I believe he became quite rich. Never sent us a penny. Never wrote. It has left me an oddball, and twisted. I'm not really into friendships. I believe people don't want me. Not really.

'My grandfather was such a wise man but he died in a flu epidemic well before his time. So he rejected me. That meant my grandmother had lost her daughter and her beloved husband, so she wanted to die to be with them. I was in the way. But she was marvellous to me. "I want to

go to them," she used to say, "but I will try and live until you are twenty, because then you will be able to look after yourself and I will try to leave you enough money to buy a house because you will be totally alone in the world." She did die when I was twenty.' That must have been when you were away in the war, I reminded her. 'Yes, I was in the Wrens. I was sitting on a lavatory in a Fleet Air Arm station in Scotland. Someone pushed a message, a telegram in its little orange envelope, under the door.'

It's left me an oddball, and twisted. I'm not really into friendships. I believe people don't want me – not really

No one can have all that happen and not be affected. And it didn't end there, for her husband left her with two children after ten years of marriage. Robin was two and Sarah six. They had no money. 'The one thing that saved me was my house. I saw it in a magazine – I didn't go to look at it – and bought it for £1,700 (my grandmother had left me £2,500). A massive house off the Portobello Road. It's flats now. It had paper peeling off the walls with great big mushrooms growing out. Nine years later when I wanted to buy a house for the children with a garden I couldn't sell it for it was still in that terrible state. I eventually sold it to a Pole who had been over here fighting in the war. He couldn't get a mortgage on it. He gave me three hundred in cash and the rest I had to trust him to send me, ten pounds a month. It saved my bacon. And he paid me to the last penny. I bought a house backing onto Epping Forest and that's when my husband flew the nest. I was lost, bothered and bewildered. Everyone around where we lived rejected me. No one wanted to know a woman on her own. I was a danger in those days.' She said she stood out like a sore finger in the prim suburbs, and would have been better off in a more working-class area.

All the time she was taking odd jobs, like looking for holes in plastic bags. And she became a postman. 'I couldn't get into acting, which is what I wanted to do, so I relieved my frustration by buying three pence worth of old china and taking it home and throwing it hard against the wall. After a while, I got into Butlin's theatres, which meant the children and I could have holidays and I could restore our health by the sea and act, which is all I wanted to do. I knew I had a rapport with the audience. They used to fall about when I played comedy.

'Then just before Christmas when I was forty-nine and selling toys in Hamleys, someone held up a phone for me.' They told her there was a young director making his first film, that it was to be improvised and that he needed a middle-aged actor to play the mother. The director was Mike Leigh and the film was *Bleak Moments*. Liz played an old woman in bed. (And now, at 85, that it is the kind of work she looks for!) That first film role was sensational; Mike Leigh gave her other parts – and that was it. 'I've never had to work in post offices or plastic bag factories again. This has wiped out my strange resentful feelings.'

And there is the writing. Liz is astonished by the popularity of her autobiography, *Our Betty*, and *Jottings*, her recent collection of short stories. She has been charmed that people call out to her on the road, 'We love you, Nana!' It has been a complete turn-around.

But she has got 'this blood pressure thing', as she puts it, and she finds herself getting very tired. 'Can't walk around much. It robs me of my energy.' Luckily she still can do readings, and she's keen to do some painting which she stopped doing a long time ago. 'And also,' Liz added, 'I have always been able to sleep at the drop of a hat. Anywhere, anytime, little naps, I grab every moment.'

What are her thoughts about death? (You can ask that question when you are getting on yourself.) 'Well, I hope the fortune-teller who told me I was going to die in my sleep is right!' Liz answered.

When I went to use the bathroom, Liz said wait until I put this CD on, 'because you can hear *everything*!' So, having already thoroughly enjoyed talking to Liz Smith, I left with a further lilt to my step to the loud strains of 'I Got Plenty of Nothing' sung by Al Bowlly.

Confessions *of an* anorak

Chris Donald's self-portrait: 'LNER locomotives should of course have four-digit numbers, not five'

Twenty years after he'd hung up his binoculars for good, **CHRIS DONALD** *was forced to confront the shameful truth – once a trainspotter, always a trainspotter...*

The other day I spotted my first train in over twenty years. I'd seen a lot of trains during that time, but not spotted them as such. There is, of course, a huge difference.

The train in question was a little red steam engine which bore the famous initials 'LNER' on its cab side. I made a note of its number, which was 54007. Anoraks among you will already be waving indignant fingers in the air. Quite apart from the fact that the London & North Eastern Railway's locomotive livery was green (or black, or occasionally blue or grey), never red, LNER locomotives should of course have four-digit numbers, not five. Even after nationalisation in 1948, the five-digit series '5XXXX' was allocated to engines of the former London, Midland & Scottish railway, not the LNER.

'For goodness sake! Can you believe that?' I said to my wife.

'What?' she asked. Her interest in trains is fairly limited, so I explained these laughable inconsistencies in layman's terms. She didn't seem greatly concerned. 'If it bothers you, why not complain to the girl on the checkout?'

We were in a supermarket at the time, and the train I had spotted was one of those coin-operated children's rides that

I stopped being a trainspotter way back in 1978. I didn't like the technological changes taking place

clutter the exits. I tutted and shook my head. If a supermarket can manage to get the 15-digit bar code right on every one of the tens of thousands of items they have on sale, surely they can manage to come up with one historically accurate train number. But years of experience have

taught me that pointing this out to a dim 16-year-old on a supermarket checkout would be a frustrating exercise at best, so I decided to let it go.

I stopped being a trainspotter – technically speaking – way back in 1978. I didn't like the technological changes that were taking place. Not in railway technology, but in trainspotting technology. Long before the arrival of mobile phones the dictaphone was making platform ends noisy and unsociable places to be. Instead of intensely scribbling numbers down in a notebook, people were shouting them into the palms of their hands. And early camcorders were being used to film passing trains which could then be spotted later on a TV screen.

The natural time to give up trainspotting would be once you have spotted every train. In the late 1950s that was nigh on impossible, with a tangled railway network and over 15,000 engines to look for. But 15 years later, thanks to the efforts of Dr Beeching and a newly installed computer system, life was a lot easier for the anorak. There were fewer than 3,000 engines at large on a much slimmer system, and anyone with access to a BR computer terminal could pinpoint the precise location of any one of them at the push of a button. (Well, five or six buttons, perhaps.)

Thus, by the age of 18, my much-travelled friend and mentor Justin had collected the number of almost every engine in Britain.

But would he stop there? Not likely. The next step is to start collecting the numbers of carriages, then coal trucks. It was at that point – when I realised that I would never find closure, and that trainspotting would be a perpetual occupation – that I decided to walk away, to rinse out my flask and hang up my binoculars for good.

Twenty-four years later I still don't feel entirely cured, and I'm sure my wife would agree. What, she will ask, is the difference between the Class 25 model railway engine she got me for Christmas, and the Class 25/3 model railway engine I now want for my birthday? And why, she will continue, must I insist on numbering all our holiday photographs on the reverse with a seven-digit number before anyone is allowed to look at them? (There is an entirely logical reason for that which I could explain here, but perhaps it would be best if I didn't.)

I believe that trainspotting was just one symptom of an underlying problem which, I fear, is with me to stay. Ano-raxia, you might call it. Or a degree of Asperger's perhaps. At the end of the day, you can take an anorak out of his anorak, but you'll never take the anorak out of an anorak. If you see what I mean.

'Hi, I'm on the game'

A woman escaped without injuries after the car she was driving ran into a hedge
Western Morning News

Northend Thistle football players held their breath last Friday as a wayward shot at goal sailed through the air towards the stained-glass windows of Brodick Church. The strike could have made a costly dent in the North-end club's kitty, not to mention a disastrous bit of damage to the church. But thankfully the ball struck the surrounding sand-stone frame and bounced harm-lessly to the ground.
The Arran Voice

An overheating lightbulb triggered a fire alarm in the City Art Gallery in York yesterday afternoon. Fire crews were not needed.
Northern Echo

COUPLE NEARLY RUN OVER
Jersey Evening Post

Fame hasn't changed Girls Aloud singer, Nicola Roberts. She ordered brown and red sauce with her chips on a recent night out at the Ivy restaurant.
The Metro

A traffic warden who once gave Sean Connery a parking ticket has retired. Sandy Bennett, of Kingussie, Invernesshire, who will be 65 later this month, has quit after 38 years.
Western Gazette

A speeding crackdown has revealed drivers are obeying the speed limit. Police held checks in Copse Lane, but the average speed of drivers was less than 30 mph.
Oxford Times

A 70-year-old man named Zheng had to sit on a sidewalk to rest after running 500 metres to catch up with a man to whom he had given wrong directions.
Henan Commercial News

An old pan used as a plant pot has been stolen from outside a house in Kirbymoorside
Malton Gazette & Herald

A Dundee reader is delighted by the fact that she has two tubs of miniature irises in full bloom at the moment. When she first saw the purple colour, she thought the flowers were crocuses. On closer examination, they proved to be irises.

George Bradshaw, 84, of Bryn Clyd, Leeswood, who lost his leg through illness, was unable to use the disabled toilet at the Golden Grove restaurant in Rossett – because it was being used as a dressing room by a Tina Turner impersonator.
Chester Chronicle

'Thousands of public artworks are springing up across the nation like giant weeds'

Towers of Babel

Why is so much public art in this country puerile, pointless and pompous?
SIMON HILLS *goes on the sculpture trail...*

This year the people of Cardiff were apparently somewhat baffled to see blocks of yellow paint daubed over the Cardiff Bay Barrage. Imagine their delight when, finally, after a few weeks, they were unveiled as a vital new piece of public art: *The Three Ellipses For Three Locks*, by the Swiss-born artist Felice Varini. The piece was made up of three concentric circles – but you could only see them if you stood in one specific spot.

Mansfield's citizens have been treated to a rather more obvious work, *High Heels* – a six-metre-high pair of stainless

steel stilettos – and, across the Bristol Channel, the artist Philip Thompson has just put the final touches to his three-metre-tall metal sculpture, titled *Heart of Stroud*, which will now sit outside Stroud College.

While the Victorians treated their citizens to public parks, libraries and museums, so today's mania for 'regeneration' is resulting in thousands of public artworks such as these springing up across the nation like giant stainless steel and fibreglass weeds.

'Local authorities park hundreds of anodyne public sculptures like tanks in

a war of cultural aggression against the relatively uneducated,' writes the artist Grayson Perry in the *Times*. 'They hope that these civic baubles will replace social capital that has been lost to decades of upheaval in patterns of work, family and leisure time.'

You can see his point. The pomposity behind these simplistic creations springing up across the nation is quite breathtaking.

Alongside a newly created pedestrian route from a viaduct in Hymers Court, next to the Tyne Bridge, for example,

They hope that these civic baubles will replace social capital that has been lost to decades of upheaval in patterns of work, family and leisure time

the people of Gateshead now have the word 'No' barking at them from five of the separate archways that form part of a railway viaduct.

'*No, No, No, No, No* is deliberately ambiguous,' according to Miles Thurlow, who created the work with fellow artist Cath Campbell. 'By giving an answer, it forces you to find a question. The meaning comes from the person who's looking at it, and not directly from the piece itself.' The work, according to Councillor John McElroy, whose official title is 'cabinet member for culture' – there's posh – 'challenges the way we think about ordinary locations'.

From Marc Quinn's statue of the pregnant, naked, armless Alison Lapper, which has been gracing Trafalgar Square recently, to the Spinnaker Tower in Portsmouth – cost: a mere £35 million – public art is local government on steroids. You think I'm a dreary functionary? Well, look at my tower, mate. Liverpool is spending £96 million on its Capital of Culture programme, including £450,000 for a sculpture by Londoner Richard Wilson – an installation that rotates an oval panel cut from the side of a derelict office block through 360 degrees.

But it's not just our urban areas that are in need of 'regeneration'. On Tiree, in the Inner Hebrides, residents have been treated to an installation, called *An Turas*, which acts as a shelter near the ferry port. Alas, it was conceived by Tiree Arts Enterprise, a group of local and visiting artists, so much of it doesn't have a roof. Nor is there a heater. Or any seats, which

seems to make it, at £98,000, rather poor value, even if it is, according to Tiree Arts Enterprise, 'a work of individuality, epic in scale, aesthetically beautiful and of contemporary and Scottish cultural significance'.

The residents of south-east Northumberland have been lucky enough to have an 'initiative' called INSPIRE, with its own public art and design officer, Wendy Stott. Wendy has rolled her sleeves up to help conceive the country's first offshore sculpture at the village of Newbiggin. The commission – part of a £10 million sea-defence breakwater scheme – is entitled *Couple* and comprises two bronze figures measuring five metres tall, which stand 300 metres out into the bay.

'My hope is that the sculpture will embody some of the emotion we all feel when contemplating the sea, the sky and the horizon,' says the artist, Sean Henry.

He shouldn't bank on it. Last year Hackney Co-operative Developments decided to uncover a four-foot-high stencil of a girl wearing a frilly dress and gas mask by the 'subversive' graffiti artist Banksy. Alas, cleaners spotted the graffiti 24 hours before the official opening in Gillett Square and removed every trace of it. Their emotional response to this great work speaks volumes for what public art really means to ordinary people.

cartoon by
M^cLACHLAN

Bio degraded

Modern biographers should pay more attention to nose-picking, says **JEREMY LEWIS**

In his last year at Oxford, Cyril Connolly spent part of his Christmas vacation in Minehead, where 'Sligger' Urquhart, the Dean of Balliol and a kindly bachelor don of the mother-hen variety, had organised a reading party consisting of himself, Maurice Bowra, the waggish and overbearing Dean of Wadham, and a team of hand-picked undergraduates. Bowra had fallen hopelessly in love with one of the group, Piers Synott, a good-looking Anglo-Irishman, and he sought to woo the object of his passion with a medley of music hall songs; but, after picking his nose throughout the rendition, the ungrateful youth told his admirer that his feet smelt, and the Dean – by now a 'broken man' – had to be taken by Sligger on a long, restorative walk through the surrounding countryside.

The music hall songs and the nose-picking are details that should spell magic to the biographer, and I fell upon them eagerly when trawling through Connolly's papers at the University of Tulsa during the course of my researches into his life. To my amazement, my rival biographer, who had riffled through the identical papers a year or so before seemed utterly unmoved by their revelations. Connolly, he tells us, 'seems to have been engrossed in Milton, Plato, Yeats and Proust' while in Minehead – and with that the reading party, freighted as it was with comicality and high emotion, is consigned to oblivion.

As Connolly himself once remarked, 'No two biographies are alike, for in every one enters an element of autobiography which must always be different,' and the relish with which I hovered over the ignoble details of Bowra's courtship may well be indicative of incurable frivolity: but my rival's high-minded refusal to tamper with nose-picking and the rest also suggests why so many modern biographies seem both inanimate and numbingly dull. Quite apart from his other qualities, good and bad, Connolly was exceptionally funny, both in print and in person, but my rival's biography is a joke-free zone. His tone is unvaryingly reverential:

so much so that after a while he wearies of referring to his subject by his surname, and calls him 'the critic' instead.

What so many biographers fail to remember is that psychological insights and the accumulation of details must be accompanied by a modicum of artistry; that the biographer, like the novelist, needs to shape his material, to interlace (if possible) the funny and the poignant, the fast-moving and the slow, the quiet and the noisy. All too often biographers are so intent on hurrying their protagonist though his paces that, like a bad host, they quite forget to introduce us to the subsidiary characters, who are bustled on and off stage without a word about their backgrounds, education, looks, proclivities or mode of dress (than which nothing is more touching and revelatory). A sure sign that the biographer has failed to make the necessary introductions comes

The relish with which I hovered over the ignoble details of Bowra's courtship may well be indicative of incurable frivolity

'Your father can't come to the phone right now, he's stuck in his ways'

towards the end of his or her labours: eager to strike a valedictory note, they tell us that old friends of their subjects are popping off – 'In July, Jim learned that his dear friend Colin had been carried off by a seizure' – but since no mention has been made of Colin until now, the emotional impact is not all that it might be.

In recent years some of our more important literary biographers have made bullish noises to the effect that we live in an age of biography, and that biography is the literary form *de nos jours*. This, I fear, is so much wishful thinking. Having come to writing biographies rather late in life, I find – to my amazement – that I greatly enjoy both the research and the writing, and find myself rocking with laughter at my own jokes as well as those cracked by my subjects (Cyril Connolly, Tobias Smollett and Allen Lane, to date), and unexpectedly moved when tragedy strikes or the time comes to shuffle off the mortal coil: but I have no desire whatsoever to read the wretched things.

Many writers, Auden among them, resent and distrust the whole business of literary biography on the grounds that it is the writer's work, not his life, that matters; and none more so than my old friend and colleague, D J Enright. He was all for my writing my memoirs, hyperbolical as they often were, but when I told him that I was writing a biography his eyes glazed over, and although he always asked me how I was getting on with it, I knew that he did so between gritted teeth, and hastily changed the subject.

For my part, I felt – and still feel, albeit more reluctantly than I did – that literary biography in particular is, for the most part, second-hand and second-rate, far inferior to autobiographies and memoirs. For all the grand claims made on its behalf, biography remains the most ephemeral of all literary forms, with Boswell and Lytton Strachey the exceptions that prove the rule; and matters aren't likely to improve so long as its practitioners continue to ignore such vital matters as nose-picking and the singing of music hall songs by lovelorn Oxford dons.

It's not a fair cop

WILLIAM KEEGAN *passed the breathalyser test every time, much to the fury of the police*

When the breathalyser was introduced, all those years ago, a judge friend said: 'Nothing to worry about. Stick to a glass of sherry, a few glasses of wine, one port and you'll be fine.' Out went the sherry over the decades, and out went the port. In came the champagne and white wine as an aperitif – and Alan Watkins's dictum that certain politicians regarded white wine as a non-alcoholic drink. Your correspondent adopted it but adapted the judge's advice, and spent many a happy hour, as it were, pondering on the definition of 'a few'. In all this time I have been stopped only five times by the police bearing breathalysers, and detect a worrying trend: the police are

becoming more and more menacing, to the point that they are in serious need of counselling.

The first episode occurred in the early 1980s when I turned left at one of those Islington streets that are two-way most of the time but occasionally light up with a 'no entry' sign for no obvious purpose. It was early evening and the policeman accepted my explanation that I had made an honest mistake, but it was Christmas

The light went to amber and stayed there. The officer could hardly conceal his displeasure

and he would have to breathalyse me. 'Blow softly,' he generously said.

The second occasion, in the early 1990s, was on the Albert Embankment when, en route late at night from Wimbledon, I was stopped at a well-known (at the time) road trap. The police were armed with a breathalyser, and pointed out that one of my sidelights was not working. Where was I coming from? they asked. 'My Greek master's funeral,' I replied. 'What have you been drinking?' 'A glass of lager with a curry.' This unlikely but genuine explanation was accepted, and the breathalyser was not applied.

Both of these episodes were handled politely and with good humour by the police. In the course of the next three episodes, however, their behaviour became more threatening. The first occasion, in the mid-Nineties, was when I was followed by a police car for about five miles in the Surrey countryside, finally hauled into a lay-by, and told that I had exceeded the thirty mph limit five miles earlier. The breath test was negative, but the manner of the policeman would not have passed muster with Inspector Barlow or Sergeant Watt.

The next occasion was in the late 1990s, when my wife and I emerged from the US Ambassador's 4th July party in Regent's Park, and the police celebrated by stopping us within 200 yards. 'Do you know why you have been stopped?' asked a very unpleasant member of the constabulary. 'No.' 'You have an out-of-date tax disc on your windscreen.' 'I also have an up-to-date one on my windscreen.' 'Have you been drinking?' 'Yes.'

It was a pretty odd type of technical offence to be displaying an up-to-date disc but to have left the old one on: to know this – they came up from behind – the two police officers must have been prowling around waiting for us. At all events, I had had only one glass of wine, and passed without difficulty. What was interesting was the unpleasant way in which the police had thought they were on to a sure thing – a diplomatic drinks party – and the sulky way in which they behaved when I passed the test.

The scene shifts to March 2004, when the family car was stopped at 1.15 am between Hammersmith Roundabout and Shepherd's Bush by a very menacing policeman, accompanied by a silent policewoman. The accusation was that I had been driving erratically and gone through three red lights.

The only erratic moment I could think of was pausing to make sure I did not take the wrong turning at the Hammersmith Roundabout, which I always find confusing. As for red lights, in common with most of us of a certain age I am appalled by the way cyclists (always) and motorists (at least half the time) cross red lights with abandon these days.

One's natural instinct, which always has to be suppressed, is to ask the police on these occasions why they are not chasing muggers or terrorists. I desisted. But I did not waste too much breath on his machine the first two times, with the result that he threatened to take me to the police station if I did not blow harder. At this stage I could not resist saying, 'Officer, this has not happened to me very often. Please tell me how to blow.'

The light went to amber and stayed there. An increasingly infuriated police officer held the machine for what seemed minutes, saying that sometimes it took a long time to turn red. But I knew I had stuck well within the judge's rules, had had four glasses of

wine between 8.30 pm and 11 pm and lots of coffee.

I passed, and the officer could hardly conceal his displeasure. 'I would drive very carefully from now on if I were you,' he said with icy politeness.

At this stage my wife pointed out that we had two children in the back of the car. 'Perhaps,' she said to the policewoman, 'you would like to come over and say hello, so that they don't grow up with the wrong impression of the police.'

I thought this was a masterstroke. The policewoman duly obliged, and we shall pass over the expression on her companion's face.

Now, the moral of this tale is simple. On all three of the more recent occasions the police should have been delighted. The point of the campaign is to impose severe limits on what the public drinks before it drives. On each occasion it was clear that the object of the law was being achieved. But the police were furious. Under the 'target' culture in which we live, they had invested time and effort in securing another offence.

But another kind of target had been achieved. They have frightened the life out of most of us, to the great financial benefit of the minicab trade. They need counselling. They should smile and say 'Well done!' when one passes the test, not make one feel like a criminal on whom the jury has been soft.

Oh, and by the way, I did not get off scot-free. A few weeks later there arrived a penalty notice, complete with photograph of my car being driven in a bus lane. Readers might like to know that on such occasions one can demand further photographic evidence. I did. But on this occasion it was a fair cop. The 'offence' had taken place earlier that same evening, with not a bus in sight.

IS ONE NEARLY THERE YET?

House Husbandry

with Giles Wood

A chucker who weds a hoarder is doomed to live in a strange and never-ending loop of junk...

Gardening lore has it that April will bring forth some 'open weather' between the showers. This antique expression refers to those precious days in which it's possible to get outside and make a start with the gardening year.

For me this means work with a bonfire at its core; and while the brushwood and other garden refuse is going up, what about the combustible material inside the cottage? Persuading Mary to part with useless detritus is a painfully slow process but I thought we had reached a breakthrough when she gave me the go-ahead to torch some horsehair mattresses (which had become eco-systems in their own right) and old computer packaging that had been gathering dust in the attic for a score of years.

Yet just as I was wheelbarrowing a load towards the crackling blaze, Mary was simultaneously staggering into the cottage with some 'bargains' from the new, 'upmarket' charity shop in Marlborough, a giant, dented lampshade amongst them ('but we could steam the dent out!') It was a case of out with the old and in with the old.

One prize was a hulking videotape of

Seven Brides for Seven Brothers.

'I can hardly wait to watch that, Mary,' I remarked.

'At least it's wholesome,' she protested. 'There's nothing but severed heads on telly these days...'

Be that as it may, when will she get a chance to

Shelf-clearing can build up a euphoric momentum – so Mary's bag-lady routine is a real spanner in the works

watch it? It took its place amid a toppling column of other unwatched video bargains including a rare biopic of the early life of Uri Geller directed by Ken Russell during his wilderness years.

Many years ago I learned to conquer the urge to buy. Just as you would resist any other uncontrollable urge – you simply wait for it to pass. It always does, usually within twenty seconds, but it certainly helps if you leave the shop. In this respect I am more highly evolved than Mary.

As well as not buying in the first place, it is a cliché of self-help manuals

that, in order to move on, spiritually, psychologically and physically, we must de-clutter. In the right spirit, shelf-clearing can build up a euphoric momentum similar to that enjoyed by Greek wedding guests in their curious plate-smashing rituals. So Mary's bag-lady routine is a real spanner in the works for, as I head for the bonfire, she will keep halting my progress with her random spot checks for 'treasures' that I might smuggle into the flames.

The quest for a weightless existence is not for her. As she saw me carrying one tea chest out of the cottage she cried, 'All documents – yes, especially school exam papers – have value. They can trigger memories or associations...'

'What about these disintegrating raffia place-mats that Freya made in Kindergarten?'

'How could you even ask such a question, you wicked warlock?' were her exact words. See what I am up against?

'What about these stale Bran Flakes?' I asked. 'Will they trigger a memory or can I chuck them?'

Drawing the curtains in our cottage often triggers a penny cascade as jars of one- and two-pence pieces are swished off the windowsills in the process. So I got myself sorted with some polythene envelopes available from most high-street banks. With both of us working on the kitchen table in a rare show of co-operation we were able to exchange the bagged copper for one organic chicken and a new spotlight for the kitchen ceiling to see what was cooking.

This positive experience seemed to have helped changed Mary's attitude towards de-cluttering. I was pleased when she supported my plan to visit the recycling centre with some ancient loudspeakers which have been biffing me in the hips for twenty years. I slipped in some pointless clothing.

Despite being middle-aged, the infantile pleasure of 'posting' things into giant letterbox shapes has not diminished. Pride of my rejects were some Pandit Nehru jackets which I used to wear until I saw myself in a photograph resembling a giant newt.

Suddenly I realised Mary was no longer in the passenger seat of our Peugeot estate. She was loading an old wooden ironing-board and some broken deckchairs into its newly vacated boot. 'We did well to come here,' she beamed.

Christmas (w)rap

by MAUREEN LIPMAN

People all around gettin' mighty restive
Money in yo' pocket 'n' yo' feelin' festive.

Every year yo' wonder how dis will go
As yo' bulk-buy tinsel and mistletoe.

Twenty-pound turkey tossed in da bath,
Gotta make appointment wiv da osteopath.

Screamin' at da kids, don't gimme dat flannel,
Stop orderin' stuff on da shoppin' channel.

And you ain't got time to draw a breath
Or to tink about da guy from Nazareth.

And de kids demand a seasonal trip
To de bearded guy in da Arsenal strip.

But dey hate the present and dey disapprove
'Cos Santa ain't fat and de reindeer don't move.

Den after Hamleys, da children's treat –
Slaggin' off da lights down Regent Street.

An' yo' folks due at nine from Newcastle-on-Tyne
But da train breaks down – snowflake on da line.

An' it's late-night cookin' and a-huffin' and a-puffin'
'Who's got da recipe fo' last year's stuffin'?'

A scream at dawn – yo' wonder wot da matter is:
Fifty-dollar robot ain't got no batteries.

So yo' smack de kids in front of visitors
An' de kids complain to their solicitors.

It's da season of peace and jubilation
Unless yo'z one of da turkey population.

All de excess food and fuss and bother
Remindin' us dat Jesus had a Jewish mother.

If da puddin' from Marks is overseasoned
She'll take it back an' she'll get a refund.

An' it's not, as da French say, cuisine nouvelle
But, please Lord, leddit be a bon Noël.

She's in a mood 'cos her Christmas wish is
Someone else offerin' to do da dishes.

Dad keeps shtum, don't wanna panic her;
Far as he's concerned, it's really Chanukah.

Grandpa's dreamin' of Brigitte Bardot
While his wife is legless on amontillado.

Den she comes out da kitchen close to tears
Like women bin doin' fo' two thousand years.

And Cliff must Carol and Cilla must sing
Another White Christmas with B-B-B-Bing.

Now da Queen is talkin' in all de wrong rhythm
In glasses an' a crown – an anachronism.

Everybody knows
Christmas is a trap.
Everybody knows
Christmas can be crap –

So everybody clap,
Let your fingers snap,
Everybody dance
To da Christmas rap.

– An' it's comfortin' to tink in da world right now
Everybody's havin' da Boxin' Day row!

The seeds of greatness

RICHARD INGRAMS *reveals the private passion of two radical reformers – for trees*

In 1974, when I was compiling an anthology of Cobbett's writings on country matters, I planted an acacia tree in my garden. I wanted to see whether everything Cobbett said about it was true. In some respects it was. The tree is certainly graceful, with a delicate white blossom in early summer. And the wood is extremely hard. But after nearly thirty years the height is disappointing – only about 25 feet by my reckoning and I doubt if it will now get any taller.

William Pleydell-Bouverie, Viscount Folkestone and later third Earl Radnor (1779–1869), was more fortunate than me. In 1824 he bought 13,600 trees, mostly 'locusts', as Cobbett called them, and planted them in clumps at his estate at Coleshill in Wiltshire and also at Longford Castle. Though many were uprooted in the hurricanes of 1987 and 1991, some are still standing today, having attained a growth of 50–60 feet.

Lord Folkestone, as he was known for most of his life, was a radical peer, one

THE ACACIA

'This is, in my opinion, the tree of trees: it was, at any rate, my desire to see this tree introduced into general cultivation in England, that induced me to import the seed and to sell the plants here'

of a handful of aristocratic lefties who played a major role in the movement that eventually led to the Great Reform Bill of 1832. He became friends with

Cobbett in the early 1800s, when Cobbett was living at Botley near Southampton and was himself busily planting hundreds of trees on his estate. Folkestone joined in many of Cobbett's crusades, such as his strenuous opposition to army floggings. 'He had an intense love of the truth and justice,' his daughter Jane wrote. 'He had a tenderness of heart, hated oppression and wrongdoing, and did not shrink from stating his views.' All this could be said with equal validity of Cobbett himself, who spent a lifetime stating his views in an endless stream of journals, books and speeches. Folkestone, like Cobbett, was impetuous and when he became an MP was urged by his father to speak with greater moderation, something he found hard to do.

'I know myself precipitate,' he confessed to his friend, and Cobbett's, William Windham.

It has been said that Folkestone was the only friend of Cobbett's with whom he never quarrelled. (This seems to be true, but it is also the case that Cobbett never fell out with Admiral Cochrane

THE SWAMP CYPRESS

'This is one of the largest trees in the world. The tree, as an object of beauty surpasses almost any other'
(THE WOODLANDS, BY WILLIAM COBBETT)

– Earl Dundonald – the swashbuckling sea-dog and himself an inveterate champion of reform.) When Cobbett was imprisoned in Newgate for libel in 1810 Folkestone regularly sent him two hares from Coleshill, and when he was later prosecuted (again for libel) in 1831 Folkestone (by now Lord Radnor) acted as a character witness.

As for the acacia trees, on his 'rural ride' in 1826 Cobbett visited Coleshill and wrote (6th September 1826): 'Yesterday I went to see them and was, for many reasons, more delighted with the sight, than with any that I have beheld for a long while.' If only, he said, they had planted acacias instead of elms – 'what a difference in the value of Wiltshire.'

He would surely have been delighted to know that, though all the elms have long since gone, a few of his trees, including a magnificent swamp cypress (see picture), are still with us.
• *Richard Ingrams's biography of William Cobbett, 'The Life and Adventures of William Cobbett' is currently out in paperback.*

The swamp cypress tree at Longford Castle sold to Lord Folkestone by Cobbett
Tree photographs by R O Kent

It was 1935, I was 21 years old and in my seventh year as a domestic servant; life as a general maid of all work had made me stupidly naïve in the ways of the world. So I thought I had gone up a notch in the servant hierarchy when I got a job as a maid in a bed-and-breakfast boarding-house in a terrace near Paddington station. Instead of the usual half-day off from 2 pm till 10 pm once a week and every other Sunday, in this job I was off every evening from 7 pm, had a key to the front door, could come in what time I liked and, best of all, I didn't have to wear caps and aprons as overalls would do. Wonderful!

There were snags: some of the men boarders tried their unwanted attentions on me and the mistress was abysmally mean with the food. She would send me to the butcher's for three pennyworth of cat's meat scraps, then pick the best bits out for her spoilt poodle and make my dinner out of the rest. She ate her main meal out in a café or fish-and-chip shop.

Recently a new boarder had taken the cheap basement room. Her name was Miss Staples but she said I could call her Lily. I began to envy her; she was a nightclub hostess and could lie in bed till midday. She was Welsh and the most amazing number of uncles, nephews, male cousins and neighbours came to London to see her. After they had gone, she sang mostly Chapel hymns. This made her very respectable in my eyes, although I had garnered the impression that nightclub hostesses were not quite respectable.

One day when I was washing the paintwork in the hall Miss Staples emerged from the basement; it was 2 pm. In a tactless moment I asked her if you had to be a bad girl to be a nightclub hostess.

'No, you don't have to be a bad girl, you can make your money on the drinks. You have to get the men to buy you pink champagne; it's only Tizer pop really – the club charges them half a crown and it only costs 2d and you get 6d commission. If you get them to drink whisky it's two shillings commission every time.'

This dishonesty didn't seem too terrible to me: from what I had seen of nightclubs on the films, the men had plenty of money. 'Do you think you could get me a job?' I asked her.

'I'll ask tonight,' she promised.

The next day she said the woman who ran the club would give me a trial. The snag was I had no evening wear. Lily was quite happy to oblige, and by eight

Fallen angels

*In her innocence, young **WINIFRED FOLEY** looked forward to a glittering career as a night-club hostess*

o'clock that evening, rouged, eye-shadowed, powdered and lipsticked, wearing one of her blue satin evening dresses, pornographically tight on my 36-22-36 figure (Lily had measured me, as I was still unaware of the significance of my curves), a pair of too small, high-heeled, ankle-strapped shoes of hers and a coney-fur cape and well splashed with Californian Poppy perfume, I tottered with her

Like a lamb to the slaughter, I followed Lily into the club room. I felt real fear when I saw the proprietress

to catch the bus in Edgware Road.

The night club was in Ham Yard, Piccadilly. I don't know what it is like now, but then it was a dreary back-street area. My illusions started to crumble. They took a bigger fall when I saw the hostesses' cloakroom, a dirty place with a fly-

blown mirror, a powder-strewn wooden table and a toilet needing a good clean.

Like a lamb to the slaughter I followed Lily into the club room. This was an improvement! A cheerful fire blazed in a grate with a number of small tables and chairs grouped around it. At the other end of the room, on a raised wooden platform, three seedy-looking musicians sat by a piano. On the wall was a life-sized painting of a naked woman. I felt real fear when I saw the proprietress, a peroxide blonde who wouldn't see sixty again, heavily made-up, with hard piercing eyes. She told me to sit on a chair in the far corner till it was my turn for a customer.

The shocks weren't over yet! The hostesses started to arrive. I had never seen anyone like them on the streets in daylight. When a woman puts her femininity on the market something happens to her eyes: they go hard and bereft of tenderness. These women looked to me like made-up corpses that came into a phoney sort of life when the club tout brought in some customers. It was a sickening tableau seeing their crude encouragement to the men to buy them drinks. I felt a mixture of pity and contempt for them, already half-drunk before they had fallen for the tout's ploy that he could take them to see a naked woman (the painting). Once inside the club the hostesses closed in for the kill. If the men had enough money they would take them somewhere for sex later.

I knew I had made a terrible mistake, but I was afraid to tell the proprietress that I wanted to leave. I caught Lily's eye and she came over to me. 'I'm sorry, Lily, but I want to get out of here. I could never do it.' 'All right, Win. I'll tell her you want to go to the lav.' When we got there the last shock of the evening came. 'I'm coming with you, Win. I'm ashamed. I should never have brought you here. Oh Win, I'm going to go straight from now on and get a proper job.'

Tearfully it all came out as we walked for the bus, me in my stockinged feet carrying the tarty shoes. Lily's father had been a miner in the Welsh valleys. He and his wife had both died from tuberculosis leaving three young children, Lily aged eight, a sister aged twelve and a thirteen-year-old brother. They were adopted by relatives, Lily by a middle-aged childless aunt and uncle. The aunt was a strict

God-fearing Chapel-goer, the uncle a shy paedophile.

He soon had Lily a terrified victim of his evil practices. One day when the aunt had gone to a Chapel concert, he used the opportunity. He was going deaf and did not hear his wife return early because she felt unwell. The shock of what she saw froze her puritanical soul. He said it was Lily that had tempted him and egged him on. She forgave neither, had Lily put in the workhouse as unmanageable and never shared his bed again.

By the time Lily was twenty she had got a job as a chambermaid in a grand hotel in London. Among the guests was a very wealthy man and his valet. The valet, a practised womaniser, took a shine to Lily. In a couple of months she was wholly under his spell. He took her virginity with the promise of marriage. Her grief was indescribable when he and his master left one day for America and he never contacted Lily again. In despair she was taken in by a Salvation Army home for fallen women. They persuaded her to have the baby, a girl, adopted. Betrayed, without means, she fell for the solution suggested by one of the other young mothers to become a prostitute. She now felt remorse and shame.

True to her word, Lily got a job as a front-shop salesgirl in a Lyons tea shop, married an elderly widower and died in her late sixties, a respectable figure. Two emotions dominated her life, regret that she hadn't kept her baby and gratitude to the Salvation Army for taking her in.

RANT

AT A RECENT social gathering, a man whom I'd always considered fairly harmless, began, quite unprovoked, to tell us about his family history researches. For the next half hour he let us have it both barrels, rudely pushing aside crockery to make room for his sprawling family tree. Now, what his sort doesn't appreciate is that fascinating as all that stuff is to them, it holds about as much interest for the rest of us as the progress of our neighbour's great aunt's ingrowing toenail. True, a spicy detail or unexpected famous name might just stem the resentment at such a ruthless conversational hijack but otherwise, eyes become unfocused and the muffled sighing begins.

As I recall, the climax of this chap's account was the discovery that his great-great-grandmother's sister ('Here she is, on the chart, Bessie; no, you're looking at the wrong one, that's her cousin') ended up in a Victorian workhouse which this party-pooper happened to have recently driven past, not knowing at the time that it was the 120th anniversary of her death!

'I could have called in,' he told us, his voice breaking, and we made sympathetic sounds, willing our host to end it all with a flourish of coffee cups and a fresh start in the sitting room.

Why don't these family historians keep their researches private and not try to share their esoteric genealogy with the rest of us? I suspect that while they can tell you their great-great-step-grandfather's date of birth, they regularly forget to send a birthday card to a brother or sister. Those TV programmes where 'personalities' trail their roots across our screens have a lot to answer for.

GRAHAM EDWARDS

'He's been a great comfort since my husband died'

ILLUSTRATION BY TOM PLANT

Charities begin at home

*When **ANTHONY PERRY'S** stepfather died, he enjoyed spending his legacy on causes which the horrible old man would have thoroughly disapproved of*

If you have a few thousand pounds to spare, don't spend it – give it away. Establish your own charity, have a lot of fun and feel like God. I did just that when my stepfather, Michael Young, died and left me some money.

The only paperwork is to write some sort of 'mission statement' – to declare what you are doing and what your 'objects' are. Ours was to reward anyone doing a bit of good in the world – but doing it without setting up registered charities with royal patrons and sending out pens that don't work. (Nothing wrong with bunging Oxfam £50 to buy more pens but we thought we could do better by seeking out the people who weren't making a hoo-ha about their good deeds or needs.)

So we established 'The Michael Young Fund', opened a bank account at Barclays and printed a background note of our origins and intentions (reproduced on the right).

He was wholly self-centred and he had no interest in anything beyond his Bible studies and the preparation of his meals

Now you may think there was more malice in my motives than a desire to become a do-gooder. It is true I wanted to scatter a bit of Michael Young's money to people he would disapprove of, but I also wanted to grope towards a wider idea of being helpful to other people. I'd always harboured an absurd desire to see the world a better place but had been thwarted by my inadequacy and laziness.

In my declining years I had read Cyril Connolly's *The Unquiet Grave* and was struck by his suggestion that there is no happiness except through freedom from angst, and that only creative work, communion with nature and helping others are angst-free. So here was a chance to help others and, perhaps, hold angst at bay a bit longer.

Needless to say, it got off to a bad start. We gave money to earnest people who were indisputably doing good – like planting trees in the Sahara desert (£500), sending poor children to summer camp (£500), a cooking stove for a drop-in centre where I had once peeled potatoes (£500) – but they were all too mainstream, worthy and obvious.

But we did eventually manage to support a few people who were doing something unlikely or who were in great need – a whistleblower blowing useful whistles on slender resources (£500), a handyman who did household repairs for incompetent old ladies (£100) and an amazing music teacher who had got the whole of a sixth-form college engaged in music – right down to a bottle band for the hopeless (£300). And a friend in financial straits (£500).

Then we found a GP who accepted as patients all those who used to be called 'the bottom of the heap' and gave her £1,000 in £20 notes to give to any of her patients who were up against it. (And we gave her the option of spending the 'grant' on a gold-plated stethoscope, but I don't think it was taken up.)

As the money started to run out we had to reduce our grants, and sometimes limited our largesse to crisp £20 notes, 'to be spent frivolously', to anyone who took our fancy:
• The Institute for Social Inventions for the proposal that all trains should

'It's like Richard and Judy but you can't hit people'

have separate carriages for massage, tea and romance.

- A bishop for a first-class 'Thought for the Day' (25 January 2001) commenting on a topsy-turvy world in which merchant bankers are paid more than nurses and City lawyers more than teachers.
- The editor of the *Spectator* for printing a particularly funny cartoon (politely accepted).
- An incompetent Cabinet minister who had been persecuted by the media – for 'Bravery Under Fire'. His secretary returned it with a humourless note.
- A grant to buy wastepaper baskets for a brave Jewish woman who had written a letter to the *Times* and was certain to be deluged with hate mail as a result.
- £200 for a very young girl with a new baby and with the father in the nick – for baby clothes, pram, etc., and generally to cheer everyone up.
- And £200 to a woman I had worked with in a slum area thirty years before who had devoted herself to the community but didn't know how to form committees and so never got any recognition. And she was still at it and sent me a thank-you card that played 'Jingle Bells' when you opened it. We made it a condition that she spent the money on herself, but I bet she didn't.

I've probably sounded a bit flippant about charity, but actually I'm quite serious. There's nothing wrong with the basic definition – 'giving to those who need it' – but how do you get a bit of cash or a bit of praise to people who wouldn't think of asking for it?

THE MICHAEL YOUNG FUND

The Fund has been established to disburse a small sum of money left to a relative (myself) by the late Michael Young who died in August 2000 shortly after his hundredth birthday.

He was not a good man. In some respects quite the opposite. He was strongly anti-Semitic, he had a deep-rooted distaste for coloured people who he feared would pollute the white races, and he propagated a mean-spirited and unforgiving interpretation of Christianity.

He paraded these beliefs under the banner of patriotism. He was a founder member of the League of Empire Loyalists and claimed, with pride, that it was he who tipped a bucket of offal over Jomo Kenyatta, at that time the President of Kenya, a member of the Commonwealth.

He corresponded with, and supported financially, Lady Birdwood and John Tyndall of the British National Party as well as various fringe religious movements. He wrote a number of poisonous pamphlets.

He was wholly self-centred and had no interest in anything beyond his Bible studies and the preparation of his meals. He neither read a newspaper nor stirred out of the house for the last ten years of his life. It is hard to find any redeeming feature in the man.

So it seems a nice idea to pass a little of the money he left to some of the individuals and the small organisations who try to do some good in the world.

'Enough! The mooing is no longer funny'

Quintessentially English

*In 2003, to celebrate the 100th anniversary of Eric Ravilious's birth, **JOHN MCEWEN** gave The Oldie a fascinating insight into the work of the artist and designer...*

The paintings of Eric Ravilious (1903–1942) present an idyllic image of English life – nature and industry, country and town, past and present in cosy and proper proportion.

Ravilious's artistic reputation rests on his watercolours – those landscapes and sparse rooms in criss-crossed weak-tea colours, the brush so dry that specks of bare paper glimmer through the paint. But he reached a far wider audience through his design work, albeit anonymously. How many cricket fans know he was responsible for the vignette of top-hatted Victorian cricketers which, until this year, was synonymous with Wisden? How many commuters looked for his signature on London Transport posters? How many English teas were enjoyed without acknowledging that he had designed the decoration on the Wedgwood china? For Wedgwood he also designed mugs commemorating the coronations of Edward VIII, George VI and, posthumously, the Queen. Left-wing friends chided him, but if he was socialist in sympathy he was also patriotic; and, though Nonconformist by background, liked 'picnics and jolly times' and even enjoyed a long extramarital affair.

He achieved his greatest prominence in 1937, when his design work was a principal feature of the British Pavilion at the Paris International Exhibition. While the Third Reich and the USSR slugged it out in crude political terms, the British upstaged such childishness with a display based on objects exemplifying England and admired for being neither modern nor dated. Ravilious was an inspired choice, his art and craft similarly suspended between present and past. He designed the catalogue, some neo-Regency chairs, the 18th-century-derived Wedgwood 'Persephone' service on which traditional

English food was served, and a display stand for tennis clothes and equipment.

Ravilious's sensibility, with its accent on form, is modernist; but his insistence on good craftsmanship and the poetic yearning of his subject matter are not. His art is a romantic compromise of the two, most influenced by Paul Nash, his teacher at the Royal College of Art, and shared with such contemporaries as John Piper and Graham Sutherland.

Ravilious, Edward Bawden, Richard Eurich, John Piper, Graham Sutherland were all born in 1903. Ravilious was closest to Bawden. They go together like a horse and carriage – similarly provincial in upbringing, fellow design students. They shared digs in Redcliffe Gardens and, from 1930 to 1932, a handsome Georgian town house at Great Bardfield in Essex. Both were meticulous craftsmen, placing the subject at the service of composition and inclining to a cool effect, emotionally restrained and limited in colour. But Ravilious is the cooler of the two, which fits his high regard for pre-Turner English watercolourists.

Watercolour was always his medium. His lack of artistic sensuality made oil paint positively distasteful. He described it as 'toothpaste'. Spare landscapes were his preference – understandably for someone brought up in Eastbourne, the downs and the sea in particular suited his linear style. His most characteristic paintings are of the downs. His nature and technique are perfectly attuned to that landscape – the pallor, the accent on form, the desiccation of his watercolours, even the chalky flicker of the bare paper. They suited his instinct for a subject where reality had a dreamlike quality, and since the downs are the most quintessentially English of landscapes, that alone assures his historical place.

He has other hallmark subjects, sometimes in tandem with the downs: contour-defining snowscapes, machinery, steam trains, night, fireworks, lighthouses and light effects in general – always more of a glow than a blaze.

When he was commissioned as a war artist, one might have doubted whether his aloof and gentle sensibility was suited to the task. Yet in the best of his war pictures – those without people – the dream memorably prevails: the flying-boats mysteriously float in the window of the sea-bleached bedroom of 'RNAS Sick Bay, Dundee'; 'HMS *Ark Royal* in Action' glows like a furnace in the dark. Death, when it came, was dreamlike too. He had always wanted to go to Iceland, 'land of the gods', and, once there, flew on a mission out to sea, never to return.

Pictured here are, clockwise from top right: 'HMS *Ark Royal* in Action'. 1940; 'The Westbury Horse', 1939; Commander Looking Through the Periscope', 1940; RNAS Sick Bay, Dundee', 1941; 'Downs in Winter', 1934; Edward VIII Coronation mug for Wedgwood; Victorian cricketers which until recently adorned the cover of the annual *Wisden*

I was a Killy Kid

At Kilquhanity House School, says **CHRISTOPHER HAMILTON**, *there was drinking, dope, bomb-making and plenty of teenage sex. Ah, happy memories...*

Education! Education! Education! If Mr Blair's earliest empty mantra seems far away, then so do the freedom and democracy I enjoyed at school; its climate of eccentric justice and forgiveness. Life at Kilquhanity was on the human scale. There, an autistic boy was embraced for his genius in mending radios and television sets. He was also epileptic: soon even the youngest child knew what to do when he had a fit and calmly did so. There were the children of Yorkshire landowners and tearaways from Glasgow estates, the offspring of lawyers, of film-makers and of an engraver of banknotes; of soldiers; of a woman who had risen to heights in MI5; of American psychiatrists and university lecturers. People still liked Americans in those days. Our farmhand had been road manager for The Incredible String Band, who gigged there once before my time.

We had our own parliament, where it was virtually impossible to lie and get away with it; where members of the community represented themselves in person; where all was defined by fluid but extensive boundaries, all relative to our sense of place and defined by a degree of respect for one another. Kilquhanity was co-educational. We had our own farm with four cows, pigs and chickens. We smoked. There was a lot of teenage sex, a bit of dope, and we made rockets and bombs. We drank. I had a twelve-bore under my bed and God kept a pretty low profile. Instead of preachiness, there was a non-judgmental sense of community.

Today, the school would be quickly labelled a 'terror cell' and soon be swarming with armed police, social workers, counsellors, shrinks and do-gooders. I suppose that there was a slight whiff of subversion from time to time, when American draft-dodgers turned up. When one pupil sent a letter to America with 'Kill Nixon the Bastard' written on its envelope, men in macs came all the way up from the US Embassy in London to interview her. I recently heard of an English state school teacher who has resorted to techniques recommended by Niccolo Machiavelli when dealing with subversive pupils. Subversive kids would have had a lean time at Killy, where there was nothing to subvert.

Today the school would be labelled a 'terror cell' and soon be swarming with armed police, social workers, shrinks and do-gooders

Kilquhanity House School was started in 1940 near Castle Douglas in Scotland by the educational pioneer John Aitkenhead. His founding motto for Kilquhanity was 'Liberty, Equality and Inefficiency'. 'Revolutions that are efficient,' he observed, 'always end up killing people.' John Aitkenhead believed that education is 'the generation of happiness'. He believed that children should be free to express their humanity in a natural way, in an atmosphere free from sexual and intellectual repression. At first, he followed the libertarian doctrine of A S Neill to the letter – until pupils voted to abolish bedtime. When he found a pupil fast asleep in a laundry basket after two sleepless nights, he successfully reasoned to a yawning assembly that bedtimes should be reinstated.

Because only democracy was compulsory, there was only one school rule:

everybody – staff, kids, farmhand, cook, etc. – must turn up for the Council Meeting. Held at four o'clock each Thursday afternoon and chaired by a kid, it was the forum for all manner of suggestions and complaints, where everybody could cast a vote. John A was frequently overruled, at times even by his own wife and children. Anything and anybody could be brought up at a Council Meeting, without fear or favour, before the entire school. 'I'll bring you up' was an effective threat in an environment where reason proved more effective than fear. If Johnny broke a window, then Johnny bought a new pane and mended it himself. Most of us became expert glaziers after a while. So tight-knit was the community that there was no need for video surveillance at Killy, and lies never survived for long in a Council Meeting. Where no conclusion could be reached immediately, 'Inquiries' would 'look into things'. With only the vaguest terms of reference, they worked in a magisterial way, so as to get at the truth. Some blurred lines existed in the sand. After a rare instance of shirt-lifting between a male member of staff and a boy, John A came out with the immortal line: 'As far as I'm concerned, mutual masturbation is okay – but I draw the line at buggery!' John was, all said and done, in some ways a traditionalist.

Because lessons were optional, several of us spent time working on local farms as tractor drivers or rough-shooting or snaring rabbits and foxes for their pelts. It follows that some of us were armed, mostly with shotguns, some with .22s and one with a Lee Enfield .303. We swapped ammo as others swapped stamps.

There were a few grey areas, I suppose, of the moral and legal kind. Several boys dealt in scrap: a couple of them enriched themselves to the extent that they could buy a car when the South of Scotland Electricity Board foolishly left a huge drum of copper high voltage mains cable lying around. Palls of smoke frequently hung over the school as insulation was burnt off whatever copper cable could be found. Some of this money went on betting.

More than one of the older boys ran accounts at bookies in Castle Douglas or Dumfries. Tobacco was usually bought from the bearded woman at Knockvennie (or 'Knockers'), a mile or two away. She sold Number 6 cigarettes one at a time at exorbitant rates. Neither this, nor the usual driving rain, could deter determined users of tobacco. In an economy drive, I once bought some War Horse chewing tobacco, ground it up and tried to smoke it. I was sick for two days.

My own first car was bought when I was fifteen. A derelict ex-Post Office Telephones Morris van with bald tyres, it had once been yellow and was now blue, except where the two had combined to make it green. It cost £8. Instead of a silencer, there was a golden syrup tin. It made a terrific noise and could be heard from miles away, so whenever I wanted to use it, I had to push it a good distance before firing up the engine. We drove it for miles – sometimes to Dalmellington, a tough mining town in Ayrshire, for dances where girls lined up on one side of the Parish Hall and boys on the other. When the last dance came (the 'creep', as it was known), the lights were suddenly turned off and there was an almighty scrum as each sex dragged their victims of choice around the back of the hall. A friend and I were once snogged then hustled outside by two trainee teachers

John Aitkenhead's founding motto for Kilquhanity was 'Liberty, Equality and Inefficiency'

from Paisley. Having the van, we were, as you might say, in pole position.

My maths career at Kilquhanity was short-lived. Asked to calculate the quantity of explosive required to remove a tree stump, I obliged and miscalculated, true to form, by one decimal place. Ten times the appropriate amount of homemade ordnance took out windows and flipped roof tiles back on themselves like playing cards. After that, bombs were 'in'. We

made half a dozen, with weedkiller, sugar, fertiliser, soap, etc. Most were let off over the course of one weekend when staffing was especially low and John A was away at an educational conference.

The largest we made employed an empty fire-extinguisher as a casing, buried in the midden next to the byre, with contact wires running out into the long grass. It went off with a soft crump that shook the ground and lifted tons of cowshit several feet into the air. Unfortunately, the cowman was entertaining the cook in his hut at the time, and as the windows came in, they were liberally soused. I shall never forget the sight of those two-tone naked figures bolting out of the door, the cook dangling bra-less,

'No, Clive, that's the fish knife'

the cowman priapic. Do not try this at home – or anywhere else. We grew out of bombs and guns after a while, when John Aitkenhead's reasoning won through. 'The thing is, son, inside yourself, you just know it was wrong, don't you?' Bottom lip quivering, I did.

Far more enjoyable than terror was copulation, of which there was a great deal, especially at the Lodge, where the older girls were billeted. That nobody got pregnant (at least during my time) is a miraculous non-conception. Expeditions to the Lodge were exciting and well-prepared. We did nonchalant recces by day, to learn which floorboards creaked; we secretly oiled hinges, locks and door-handles and furtively hid assault ladders in the undergrowth beneath windows. We 'borrowed' staff keys and cut doubles. Those most prized were for larders and storerooms, from which we raided industrial quantities of breakfast cereal, bread, jam, honey, coffee and tea, potatoes and hid them behind false panels in the lofts of our rooms. Girls occasionally came to see us, but the first move was usually left to us. Many of the first steps in courtship, however, were innocent, tender and intense. Going on a 'Midnight Walk' was often a key moment. Would she still hold your hand in the dark after you had helped her over the stile at Square Point? Whether they were in high summer or in bitter moonlit frost, those were moments I shall never forget.

'Useful Work' had to be undertaken by everyone, kids and staff alike, for 45 minutes after breakfast. Mopping, washing up, recycling rubbish, lighting fires... My own chores were lighting the staff-room fire and collecting the cows from a field three-quarters of a mile away.

What did we learn, apart from trapping, farming, epilepsy, commodities trading, glazing, building, boat-building, bomb-making, autism, driving, shooting, fucking, democracy, etc.? Though a committed Scots Nationalist, John Aitkenhead was an inspired teacher of English. He brought alive George Mackay Brown, Shaw, Wilde, Orwell, Wells – even Bertrand Russell and Homer Lane. He read us Sassoon and Owen, R S Thomas and Robert Graves. Chris Grieve (Hugh MacDiarmid) and Zelda were friends of the Aitkenheads and sometimes came to visit. When one boy created his own alphabet, John learned it so as to correct any mistakes his pupil made and gradually taught him the conventional one. John took an interest in dyslexia long before it became a fashionable concept, when one of his own children had difficulty in reading and writing. Asked how he cured him within a few short months, John replied: 'I just took him on my knee and read with him.'

The only educational trips during my time were to the Gorbals and the slaughterhouse in Castle Douglas. Swimming was in the River Urr. Camping trips to the north of Scotland were magical. Lessons and lectures were given by a wide range of talent: Anne Reidpath taught drawing and Mr Douglas Lees, a card-carrying CPGB communist from the Auchencairn Spar shop (where everything was twice the price), argued for the nationalisation of land. We all voted against. Football was played on what remained of the lawn, and refereed by Jody, a (by my time) snappy and arthritic border collie.

One winter, we found a swan that had flown into an electricity cable and been decapitated. We took it back with the intention of eating it; then some vague idea came into our heads that swans all belonged to the Queen and that we, in turn, might be beheaded if we did so. So we wrote to Buckingham Palace and sat back to wait. After a couple of weeks, when the swan was pretty high and no reply had come from the Fount of Honour, a decision had to be made. In true Killy style, we put it to the vote. That week, food had been especially poor, so we decided unanimously to eat it.

The skin practically fell off. We cut away those parts in the most advanced state of decomposition and spit-roasted what remained on the site of our annual midsummer bonfire, with baked potatoes cooked in the embers. It was extremely unpleasant: fishy in flavour and with surprisingly little meat. Several weeks later, we received a letter from the Royal Household telling us that, as the unfortunate creature was already dead, we had better eat it. This was our only contact with the British Establishment.

Large dinners were occasionally cooked by night, and in secret, in the kitchen, which we accessed with duplicate keys. As an Aga gives off no smell from its oven, and we blacked the windows out, these usually went unnoticed. But once the pheasant, or duck, or rabbits, came out of the oven, aromas began to circulate. More than once, we took pity on a starving young female member of staff. She readily swore herself to secrecy.

Perhaps inevitably, my own son has taken a different course. He is in the upper-sixth form of a good public school, has his heart set on a military career, is Head of III Form, a Prefect and rows for his College. Having been presented with the Sword of Honour, he is RSM of his Combined Cadet Force. I am exceedingly proud of him and of all that he represents. At the same time, after Mr Blair, like a brownshirt in a clockmaker's on Kristallnacht, vandalised 600 years of parliamentary democracy – and, on the coat-tails of a globalised insecurity industry, gleefully trashed our civil liberties with his Civil Contingencies Bill – I feel mildly privileged to have had education, education, education: to have been, and to remain, a Killy Kid.

'This always happens when you meet up with someone from Friends Reunited'

IKEA
ARK
INSTRUCTIONS

Cartoon by

MCLACHLAN

Washed away

With sea levels rising and fears abounding about storm surges, **BARRIE de LARA** *recalls being a child caught up in modern Europe's worst-ever weather disaster*

On the night of 31st January 1953, an enormous storm surge was created in the North Sea, after a strong northerly gale piled up an already exceptionally high tide in the Wash. Spilling southwards, it broke sea walls in more than a thousand places along 1,000 miles of the coast of England and the Netherlands. In England, 367 people died – 64 of them my neighbours on Canvey Island, in Essex – and 200,000 acres of farmland were rendered unusable for years, with some never being recovered. In addition, some 20,000 buildings were damaged.

The entire population of our small island, about 7,000 at that time, had to be evacuated. The place looked bizarre. Today it is densely populated and looks like an extension of nearby Basildon, but in the early Fifties there were few inhabitants and it was still quite rural. Many people, such as my grandparents, lived in houses that were basically wooden shacks. Until 1932, when a second-hand bridge was bought from the City of Liverpool Corporation, the only access to the place, unless you had your own

The water was cascading, roaring – four or five feet high – through the front door of our one-storey home

water transport, was by means of a rowed ferryboat, or by stepping-stones at low water. It was the greatest weather disaster in modern European history.

My mother woke me by bursting into the bedroom I shared with my brother. She stood me up on my bed and dressed me, rapidly pulling trousers, jumper and school rain- coat over my pyjamas. I sat down to reach for the *Teddy Tail* annual I had dropped when I fell asleep and found it soggy and swollen, floating in improbable water. I was confused and even slightly amused, but certainly not frightened. Someone – most possibly my father – said, 'We're being flooded!' Water was cascading, roaring, four or five feet high, through the front door of our one- storey, jerry-built home. My brother, older than me by ten years, earned my lifelong respect by standing up to his knees in water in front of a mirror and putting on a white shirt and his Essex County Cricket Club tie. 'If I'm going to drown, then I'm going to drown decently dressed,' he announced to us all.

There was a scramble for the roof space. Father hauled himself up through the trapdoor. Then mother climbed onto my brother's shoulders and was manhandled aloft. I was passed up like a package. Last came my brother, muttering that he knew exactly what had happened: 'People have been saying it for years. The sea wall at Tewkes Creek crumbled away.'

Our sea defences had last been upgraded by Dutch engineers in the 17th century. We perched in the rafters like roosting hens, while the North Sea engulfed my world. The loft was quite extensive for a bungalow-cottage and had one large window under the eaves, to give the impression of an upper floor that we

We picked up a thin, exhausted man, who was naked. They put him on the seat next to me, wrapped in a blanket

did not in fact possess. It was dark, and after an hour the electricity supply failed. We lit candles and heard dull thuds – as windows burst inwards – as well as some screaming and shouting.

My father had grabbed two cylindrical tins of Player's cigarettes, a bottle of rum, a pack of cards and matches: you could tell he was an ex-Navy man. My mother had collected candles, money, her fur coat and jewel box. My brother had taken his best shoes and his cricket bat.

A mile away, in his wooden shack, my grandfather had quickly moved his collection of illegal firearms and ammunition boxes above water level. Just what that level might be, none of us knew for sure and my father busied himself with working out how to break through onto the roof, until my brother pointed out that the sea would have to rise thirty feet above what was usual at this time of the year to make that necessary. In fact, by three in the morning, the tide was at least forty feet above the normal level at London Bridge.

When it appeared that the water was not going to rise any further – it stopped at about two feet below the trapdoor – we relaxed a little. We breathed more easily when it began to drop: the tide was on the turn. When the top of the kitchen

stove was uncovered, my father waded up to his armpits into the kitchen and made us all cocoa. The gas had continued to flow throughout. I wriggled my way over to the window and, as the dawn broke, I saw many strange things.

Floating past the window was a kitchen table, upright, with plates and glasses and a clock on it. Then came odd bundles of cloth; a pig-sty, listing badly, with dead pigs in it; a flock of quacking farmyard ducks, followed by a semi-submerged radiogram bobbing against the sill and a wooden box full of shoe-brushes. Great plumes of flotsam floated out to sea, some of it as far as the Nore, near Sheerness. We were hailed by a motor-cruiser, its engine grumbling. The crew said they would take me, but my mother said that we would all go together. Other boats passed, including one old fishing smack under beautiful red-brown sails. In the end it was the Army that rescued us, in huge lorries with vertical exhausts. Water covered the landscape and there was no way of telling what was road and what was field, so my brother sat on the bench seat in front and directed the driver.

We picked up a thin, exhausted man, who was naked. They put him on the seat next to me, wrapped in a khaki blanket. He said nothing, but his lips trembled a little. I was fascinated because his face was billiard-chalk blue.

After a while the soldier looked at our companion and pulled the blanket over his face. 'This bloke's a goner, Corp,'

he said. My mother put her head in her hands and howled. It had only been a few years since her home in London had been destroyed by the Luftwaffe. She had seen dead people before. I never had – I was eight years old.

Trains from the station two miles away, just off the island, were still signalled mechanically and hauled by steam engines, and they were largely unaffected. Parts of the line were flooded, but the trains continued to puff to London, where we ended up many hours later – at an aunt's house. By then thousands of refugees, clutching pathetic possessions, were front-page news.

We could not return for five weeks. When we did, my father rowed me down our lane in a 15-foot boat, which he moored to the gatepost. There were still five feet of water over our part of the island at high tide and the house was a stinking mess. Virtually nothing could be saved and almost nobody was insured. Had it not been for the fund inaugurated by the Lord Mayor of London, Sir Rupert de la Bere – my grandfather's commanding officer in the First World War – and foreign aid, thousands would have been left destitute. Our community has vanished and the area is still eight feet below sea level.

Historically, storm surges have occurred with regularity. The Norfolk Broads were created overnight by one in the 14th century. Given rising global sea levels, a storm surge could push a spring tide up to Ely or even Cambridge. I do wonder what contingency plans exist.

Opposite, main picture: 20,000 buildings were damaged in the flood along 1,000 miles of coastline, and for weeks after could only be reached by rowing boat, inset Right: the flood destroyed 200,000 acres of farmland which remained unusable for years afterwards

When Larry met Dorothy

TRADER FAULKNER *discovered that his rival for the affections of the beautiful young actress Dorothy Tutin was none other than Laurence Olivier. The plot thickened...*

The London theatre establishment was a pretty austere challenge when I arrived at Southampton on a one-way ticket from Sydney one chilly May morning in 1950. With £12 in cash left, my security was the unquenchable optimism of a twenty-year-old. A stint in the kitchens of Lyons Corner House was followed by an audition for the then reigning monarch of London theatreland, H M Tennant, which resulted in my playing the Richard Burton role on

'You bastard,' I thought. 'The bedfellow of Vivien Leigh scavenging like a fruit fly on the woman I adore'

Broadway in John Gielgud's production of Christopher Fry's *The Lady's Not for Burning*. Back in London, in his production of *Much Ado About Nothing*, I met and was bewitched by a young actress

soon to be acclaimed as the successor to the ingénue legend, Maggie Albanese. It all seemed too good to be true.

The piquant and elusive ingénue who cast a seven-year spell over me was Dorothy Tutin, soon to become an outstanding success in Graham Greene's *The Living Room*, and a passionate idyll blossomed on holiday on the isle of Arran. She confided her need for independence from her possessive parents and was looking for a bedsit in London. Houseboats were becoming the rage, so

I suggested one. 'Darling Trader, that's genius!' I was embraced but not kissed. She bought one in Chelsea and I rented a floating snuggery almost next door.

An offer to play Malcolm to Olivier's Macbeth and Sebastian to Vivien Leigh's Viola at Stratford-upon-Avon was an opportunity I couldn't refuse. On the afternoon of *Macbeth*'s opening night, over a Guinness in the actors' pub, The Dirty Duck, a stranger asked me if I would deliver a personal note to Sir Laurence Olivier. He handed me a plain calling card: the handwriting was Dorothy's, and it was a warm and loving good luck message. I'd received nothing.

I'd once confided my feelings about Dorothy to the avuncular Olivier, and

now I realised that he was my rival in love. 'You bastard,' I thought, 'the bedfellow of one of the most beautiful women in the world, Vivien Leigh, scavenging like a fruit fly on the woman I adore.' I tore back to confront Olivier in his dressing-room. He read the card, said nothing, but sat me down beside him.

As Vivien Leigh's twin in *Twelfth Night* I had to wear a nose identical to hers: made from nose putty, it always resulted in my resembling a poor man's Cyrano de Bergerac. Olivier scooped a blob of undertaker's wax from his make-up tray and, with the small wooden spatula he'd used to mould so many famous characters' noses, fashioned me a perfect retroussé identical to Vivien's. Holding it aloft like a jeweller appraising the Koh-I-Noor diamond, he thrust it into my hand: 'Here, baby, keep it and learn how to do a proper nose.' Then, 'Christ, baby, out quick! It's curtain-up in seven minutes.'

I was stumbling up the stairs clutching the historic spatula before I realised. Clever move! Game, set and match to Olivier. 'All right, maestro!' I thought. 'You'll keep till next time.'

Back on my houseboat, the Stratford season ended and my relationship with Dorothy on hold, I learned from the nightwatchman, Ben Bowyand, a lizard-eyed mischief-maker who knew everybody's business, that Dorothy was receiving nocturnal visits from Larry, and that he would be visiting her that night. So I put a long-anticipated plan into action.

On the pontoon, near the top of Dorothy's gangway, was a huge, disused garbage bin with two small holes where a handle had been torn off. I climbed in, armed with an empty wine bottle, pulled the lid down and waited, using the holes to peep through. Sure enough, around midnight, Larry arrived, knocked furtively, and disappeared down the hatch of Dorothy's houseboat.

The January night was icy, and at one stage I had to get out to restore circulation. As I was stretching my legs, a Daimler pulled up on the opposite side of Cheyne Walk, and out stepped what looked like a very classy whore in a leopard-skin coat. 'She's obviously here to service him after he's finished with Dorothy,' I reckoned, but after walking up and down for a bit, obviously fed up and frozen, the whore drove off.

I returned to my vigil, replaced the bin lid, and waited. At last he emerged, fondly embracing Dorothy. I rose and stepped out with the bin lid on my head. Dorothy, glimpsing this apparition across Olivier's shoulder, shot back down her hatch, as he made his way myopically up the gangplank. I moved in, ready to deliver the coup de grâce with my bottle. He saw me and stopped dead. There, in a glimmer of moonlight, stood an exhausted old man in a pin-stripe suit, bowler hat and canary-yellow gloves.

In an instant this instinctive performer seized the moment. 'Baby, baby,' he crooned, unshaven, moonfaced, vulnerable. Loving and forgiving, I was lost.

I tossed the bottle behind me into the Thames and flung out both my arms.

'Oh Larry, how lovely to see you,' I said, and there we swayed, clasped in a silent embrace on the rocking pontoon.

'Baby, what are you doing here?'

I floundered and lied desperately. 'I'm about to play a murderer on TV, and I'm getting into character.' He took my face between his hands. 'Well, let me tell you. You're a very convincing murderer. You're going to be wonderful in the part. A definitive lunatic, baby!' He kissed me on both cheeks. 'I've got to go. I see my car's waiting.' Off he went, blowing me another kiss as he disappeared. It had begun to snow and I simply stood there.

Years later, at a dinner party given by Vivien Leigh shortly before she died, I told this story. Vivien knew about Larry and Dorothy. Her expressive face was a study. 'Oh, Trader! Jealousy was crucifying both of us. The leopard-skin "whore" on the Embankment was me.'

Pictures, from left: Dorothy Tutin; Trader and Vivien Leigh with matching noses; Olivier as Macbeth; Trader and Tutin

'Get me a life'

To war, with sketchbook

Artist **JOHN WARD** *landed in Normandy on D-Day, pencil and paper at the ready...*

Seeing so many soldiers on telly recently reminds me of my six years and four months of inglorious service with the Royal Corps of Engineers, 1939–1946. Because of my training at the Royal College of Art, where a knowledge of architectural drawing was compulsory, I became a draughtsman in the REs. I spent the first two years digging, lifting, learning about knots and lashings and the ways of pontoons. I was totally unsuited to any kind of military responsibility and being the lowest of the low afforded me time. There was time to read and time to draw – and subjects were plentiful. Few of my fellow-soldiers had come across someone who could draw their portraits, design birthday cards for their 'loved ones' (I can hear the scorn those soldiers would have had for that treacle phrase) or colour their wedding photos. I became a useful member of my section.

When I was eventually drafted to an HQ to work as a draughtsman, it was

to the 3rd Infantry Division, destined to lead the assault on Normandy. I landed on D-Day after a night of violent sea-sickness – the mixture of a supper of tinned pork and sea-sickness pills hadn't been very happy. But bang on time I was there on the beach at 11.30 in the morning, wet and totally recovered. In my pack were paper and pen, ink and pencils, and on the evening of the next day I made my first drawing.

Soldiers have an amazing ability to 'settle down'. No matter what the circumstances and no matter what odd things were going on I was expected to continue drawing – and what subjects I had!

Half a mile away, across a large area, were the remains of the gliders which had ferried the airborne troops. These abandoned monsters lay at all angles, in all conditions. Some were quite smashed up, laying bare their fragile construction – and there was not a soul about. There were three very special ones in which the Ox and Berks Light Infantry troops had travelled to capture the first bridge. Wonderful subjects.

While Henry Moore was cribbing the sleeping disciples from Mantegna's 'Agony in the Garden' for his Underground sleeper drawings, I was doing the

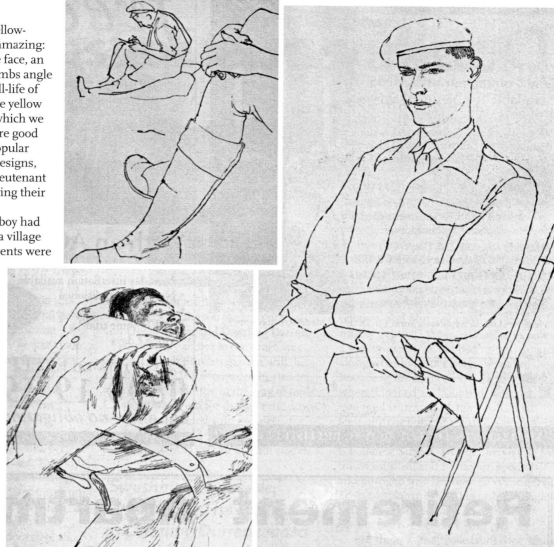

same for my sprawling fellow-soldiers. Men asleep are amazing: all pretence falls from the face, an innocence appears and limbs angle themselves oddly. The still-life of kit, boots, packs, rifles, the yellow stuff of parachutes with which we lined our slit trenches were good subjects. I made a very popular sheet of possible latrine designs, and sketched the spare Lieutenant Colonel and Adjutant having their morning bucket wash.

A ten-year-old French boy had been killed by gunfire in a village without a camera: his parents were avid for some record, so would I come and draw him? This led to my meeting the grande dame of the village, who gave me a glass of wine (thank God it wasn't the local cider) and an old sketchbook which she had had in Paris. In it I sketched my way through France, Belgium, Holland and Germany.

I see on the news that British soldiers are commended for being friendly easily with the locals, and this was so during the war. We hoped to get our feet under their tables, and

drawing the children was a good start.

Soldiers were an interesting lot: the REs comprised every kind of technician, lightermen from the Thames, doctors from the industrial North, plumbers, masons, carpenters, builders, mechanics of every kind. And how eloquent they were: an insurance agent from Liverpool who travelled around on a bike collecting half-crown insurance contributions was so vivid a story-teller that I dug his slit trench so that the stories should not be interrupted.

It was like inhabiting a picture by Brueghel with Hieronymus Bosch to hand. In its way, no bad corrective to the years of art education at the Royal College of Art.

Scenes of wartime life from John Ward's sketchbook – including (top right) 'Capt Boyce MC, intelligence officer' and (left) 'Signals Sergeant, much disliked

Donkey business

A really cute ass, full of Eastern promise – how could **DUNCAN FALLOWELL** *resist?*

Some years ago the Princess Beris Kandaouroff said to me, 'You should interview my friend, the Queen of Egypt.' So I went to Cairo. The Queen – Farouk's first wife – was a melancholy delight, and after I'd done her, the Pyramids and Tutankhamun, there were a few days to kill, so I asked the hotel for a guide. Suleyman was fifty, fat and bald, but eager and knowledgable. 'Call me Sully,' he said. I ordered a car and we sped off.

First on my list was plain white cotton sheets and pillowcases. We must have ransacked every emporium in the best shopping district. Out came the cellophaned packets, pile upon pile, in cotton of every colour including white. But all the sets were embroidered. I didn't want embroidery. I wanted plain. Impossible. Sully couldn't understand why I was so put out by embroidery. For him embroidery was pukkah. Second on the list was the City of the Dead. Sully showed me his family tomb, a small mud-coloured mausoleum with dead snakes inside. He said, 'I shall finish here. And my wife. And my three sons.' We reflected on mortality for a minute or two, then he asked, 'Where next?'

'I'd like to go to a *hamam*.'

'You mean a Turkish bath?'

'Yes. A beautiful old one.'

'Are you sure? Maybe you do not understand. I mean *hamam* no good for you.' He drew closer and said, 'Because *hamam* is for man like go with man. I must tell you this because it may be dangerous for you.'

'Why dangerous?'

'Even they could rape you.'

'You can defend me. I'm so hot and sticky. Do you know of one?'

A metallic glitter had crept into his eye. 'I know of many *hamam*. But if you like go with man I come to your hotel room right now!'

'What?'

'*Hamam* boys are dirty. I am clean man.'

'Yes, I can see you're clean.'

'I have big machine.'

'Can we have another go at those sheets? How about the bazaar?'

Because of Islam's prohibition of just about everything, a healthy Egyptian male is desperate for sex with just about anything – so long as it's a secret. It seems that the wrath of Allah is only for the honest. The difficulty was in me – I didn't fancy Sully. Back at the car the

MR FALLOWELL

'My friend in village south of Cairo, he have very beautiful donkey. With long eyelashes...'

driver had switched on Arab pop music. In a razzle of syncopated wails we drove to the Khan-el-Khalili Bazaar, where again we hit the embroidery problem. A women of breathtaking obesity waddled past in pantaloons. Sully said, 'See what she is doing with her hips? That means she like it by the back door. Life is very short. A man must taste everything. We go to your hotel now?'

I pretended to examine some jute sacks, piles and piles of them, all identical. The shopkeeper raised two desultory eyes above a hookah, pulled out the mouthpiece, but Sully waved no, no, and whispered to me, 'What you like doing? What you do first?' Now that the driver wasn't with us, he was getting bold.

'After kissing, you mean? You're very curious.' He wanted me to be lascivious

– what the hell. 'Licking...' I said, and a dreamy look came over his sweating face.

'I like licking too!' he enthused. 'Girls are not easy to find in Egypt so boys are very popular. I have an idea. I come to your room. You feel my machine. If you don't like, I go. If you like, I don't go. I have big machine.'

'Yes, you said. So do I. The thing is, Sully, you aren't my type. I go for younger. I know it's shallow of me but –'

'My eldest son. You can be his friend! He likes English...'

Gawd. I could just see Dad jumping on the two of us. Dear Sully... a nice friendly middle-aged Egyptian desperate for a bonk. He realised I was digging in and now played his trump card. 'You like donkey?'

At once he detected a slight change in my expression and knew he'd hooked my curiosity. 'In Egypt we have saying: "You have big machine, you bang donkey. You like big machine, donkey bang you." Many men like play with donkey. You like to try donkey?'

'Yes, I would.'

'You would?'

'Why not? I've never had a donkey.'

'Ah, this is wonderful. My friend in village south of Cairo, he have very beautiful donkey. With long eyelashes. I contact him and telephone you tomorrow.'

Tomorrow is Army Day and I'm watching *The Dam Busters* in my hotel bedroom. It isn't dubbed and Arabic subtitles are scrawled across the screen from right to left. The phone rings. It's Sully. 'When you go back to London?'

'Tomorrow.'

'Oh, oh, oh.' Sully is moaning like a sick bear. 'My friend is away. He is back in two days. Can you change your ticket?'

'I can't, I'm afraid. What a shame.'

'This is very sad. But Sully give you promise. Next time you are in Cairo we will make something beautiful with a donkey. Okay?'

'That's very sweet of you, Sully. Thank you. God bless.'

I have yet to return.

ILLUSTRATION BY ARTHUR ROBINS

BORE TV
(See Digital Channel 356)
This week's highlights

❖ OFF THE BEATEN TRACK **NEW SERIES**
Monday 8.45pm, Bore TV

Continuing his exploration by motorbike of the little known highways and byways of Britain, actor Yonty Marsden (of *Life with the Littlewoods* fame) visits a Garden Gnome museum in Port Talbot, a teashop run by a former Wimbledon umpire and a one-time nuclear shelter in the Pennines that's been converted into an organic mushroom farm. **(S) (145132)**

❖ OUR BURIED HERITAGE
Tuesday 7.30pm, Bore TV

It is day 27 of the Walsingham Down dig and there is still nothing to confirm Professor Beard's theory that this was once the site of a huge Roman temple dedicated to the goddess Venus. Hopes are dashed when the tiny metal fragment unearthed last month turns out to be part of a discarded motorbike exhaust. Meanwhile, the Professor's students are constructing a 3-D computer model of what the temple may have looked like. Presenter: Martin Moulsdale.

(S)(145132)

❖ SAVING THE PLANET
Wednesday 8pm, Bore TV

The team is in Lincolnshire visiting the only surviving peat bog in England – home to one of the rarest insects in the country, the elusive water-ant, whose habitat is being threatened by modern drainage schemes. Cilla meets local wildlife expert Roy Wildersleeve and films the thriving colony of ants. Also: building a bat sanctuary with Clive Borage. **(S)(155832)**

❖ ALL-TIME TOP 100s!
Thursday 10.30pm, Bore TV

Jimmy Carr counts down the all-time Top 100 'Top 100' programmes. Will 'Top 100 clips of second-rate comedians saying how great the 1970s were' beat 'Top 100 put-downs from *Newsnight Review*' or 'Top 100 *Eastenders* Slanging Matches'? **(S)(145442)**

❖ THE PROPERTY LADDER
With Kate Manners and Willie Slate
Friday 9.30pm, Bore TV

Long-time partners Miles and Jeremy seem to have found the country cottage of their dreams – until their surveyor steps in. PLUS a loft conversion can put £££ on the value of your property. But there are snags, as Maidstone couple James and Hannah discover to their cost. And moving to Bulgaria – the pluses and minuses. **(S)(905132)**

❖ CAMCORDER NATION
Friday 11pm, Bore TV

Yet more hilarious clips of old people falling off chairs, middle-aged people falling over at weddings and children falling over in gardens. Has anyone in your family been caught on camera falling over? Send us your clips and each one shown could earn you £12. **(S) (145132)**

❖ DID YOU JUST SEE THAT?
Saturday 10pm, Bore TV

A panel of teenagers discuss the programme that was on just before this one. **(S) (146632)**

PICK OF THE WEEK

❖ DECISION
Wednesday 9pm, Bore TV

Maggie and Walter have still to decide on the right colour of paint for the spare bedroom. Maggie favours a neutral cream, but Walter has set his heart on a brighter shade of pink to go with the orange curtains. A visit to the local DIY store ends in a stalemate. Now, Walter's mother is due for a weekend visit. Who will she support – or will she propose a totally different colour? **(S) (145132)**

Temple Garden

SKETCHES OF JAPAN

*Regular Oldie cartoonist and illustrator, **MARTIN HONEYSETT**, recently returned from two years as Visiting Professor of Western Cartooning at Kyoto Seika University in Japan. He was their first ever Western lecturer. Here he shares his vivid and insightful impressions of this fascinating country as only a cartoonist can*

LEFT: Sketch of a 'salaryman' (a Japanese colloquialism for a white-collar male company employee) – 'even the "salarymen" have little round-eyed animals hanging from their phones...'

A well-ordered people...

Yakuza gangsters, known for their elaborate tattoos and severed little fingers.

Autumn leaf viewing

Pachinko parlours, 'where people appear to be addicted to fluorescent lights, loud music and the incessant clatter of the pinball machines'

Festivals are everywhere – as are those taking pictures with their mobile phones

Jumbo Tosses a willing local.

The great white elephant

Looking out over a beach in Mozambique, **WILLIAM ATHILL** *saw a huge white man struggling with a small blue boat. It was his introduction to an extraordinary character*

Some years ago I was standing on the veranda of my shack in Mocimboa da Praia mulling over what I could do to hinder the proliferation of the timber trade in northern Mozambique. The sun had just trawled up over the horizon and the offshore breeze carrying all the delicious dewy morning scents of the African hinterland had died down gently to nothing. The fishing fleet, I imagine one of the last fishing fleets under sail, was lying before me, sixty wooden sailing ships becalmed, their multihued sails hanging limp in the dead morning air. The smell of the fishermen's charcoal braziers and the easy confidential sound of their talk, calling between boats, came clearly to me across the still waters.

I recalled only too clearly that when young I too had worked a shark netting dhow out of Watamu in Kenya. We sailed out into the night, out onto the north Kenya banks, and there in the empty vastness of a darkened sea we shucked the net, a huge drift net that streamed out half a mile from the bow .

I would go with Jumbo to the Makonde gatherings. They would line up to be thrown into the bush by him

Every night we were carried on the bosom of the prevailing current – no engine, no sail, just an open boat and three men. Every now and again a freighter would appear, its lights like a city coming up over the horizon. We would light a guttering paraffin lamp and argue about whether they would see it or not, the throb of its engines coming louder through the waters and through our hull and through our very minds, our hearts in our mouths until the beast was pounding and throb-

bing past and on its way. Relief would then again give way to the chill darkness of a fish-noise whale-broached night.

Anyway, there I was on the veranda daydreaming when suddenly a commotion on the beach caught my eye – a huge white man and a little blue sailing dinghy. The huge white man was struggling with his mast, surrounded by a growing crowd of naked children. He raised the mainsail and the children cooed in wonder at the lettering and numbers on the sail which said 'E12'.

There was a twang and the mast fell over. The floundering sail trapped a mass of children beneath it who squealed in amusement, and the huge white man slowly started again.

The wind gathered, as did the sea, and a small swell fell on the white and sandy strand. It was about midday. The huge white man and now his crew of two-score naked children launched the blue boat amidst great hilarity into a freshening blow. The sail flapped, the boom clanged like a tinny bell off various heads, and the huge white man flopped over the gunnel and into his boat. A ragged cheer went up.

The huge white man stood up and heaved on the mainsheet and the sail tautened; the little blue boat with a bone between her teeth crested a swell prettily; the huge white man's hat blew off and the beach crowd clapped – twang went something and the mast and the huge white man fell over into the sea.

The beach crowd fell about and many started doing spontaneous somersaults on the beach. Others plunged into the sea to haul and help the little blue boat up onto the beach. I walked down to ask the huge white man to lunch.

'Hello, that's a pretty little boat. Not many like that here.'

We both looked out over the Indian Ocean, hoping, I suppose, to see the Hamble or perhaps Morston Regatta come beating around the headland. They didn't, and our eyes met. His were mild and heavy-browed; he looked a bit tired.

'No, it's an old Enterprise, you know – not in great shape, it's true to say.' It was true: the boat was being hauled out of the sea by a multitude of under-elevens. It reminded me of a nature film in which a black carpet of safari ants is seen carrying away a dead and crushed locust.

'Pity.'

'I brought it down from Lake Malawi.' (Over 800 miles away across desert, mountain range and swamp.) 'Maybe Bora beetle.'

'Maybe.'

I wondered at this huge man with his head hung down and sea water streaming down his cheeks.

'Do you know, I came down here to have a relaxing sail to get away from Mueda and the bush and to get away from my work. I should have checked. I should have known they would steal all the shackles.'

I hate bitter conversations about how things always get stolen in Africa: they are depressingly familiar and lead to nothing but people talking about how they hate being where they are, so I said what every Englishman says when confronted with something he doesn't want to address: I said, 'I am sorry.'

He sighed.

I thought I would cheer things up. 'What are you doing in Mueda? It's so lovely and cool. I love Mueda.'

'My wife and I work for the Church. We are missionaries.'

Bugger, I thought, perhaps a trifle uncharitably, the only Englishman in 28,000 square miles and he has to be a missionary. Not going to be much fun hunting buffalo with some weirdo gooder Terry Waite lookalike. Even more gloomily, into my mind's eye jumped Maugham's Mr Davidson from *Rain*.

'Are you still trying to convert the Makonde tribe?' I asked, a bit harshly. 'Surely the Portuguese would have given that a good stab.'

'We are not really converting types. Ruth and I are translating the Bible into the Makonde language, but it is difficult as Makonde is not really a written language. We have been here seven years, our son was born here and we have only just completed Deuteronomy... Oh, we are also helping to build a hospital, but they keep stealing the roof.'

We both looked down at the puddle of water spreading around his huge feet. One sandal was missing.

'By the way, my name is Jumbo, Jumbo Wilson. We are lucky in a way,' he smiled. 'The Makonde are charming people, perfectly godless and broadly illiterate, I agree, but then, you see, our mission cannot be accused of being aimless.'

He was, as I would get to know later, being gentle and generous, because I knew the Makonde; they certainly were not godless – they had masses of gods and spirits and devils and carried them openly through life. If you want a guard in northern Mozambique you employ a Makonde because they are good at murdering people with their poison arrows; they are good at poisoning. They are very small, covered in tribal scarification and primitive tattoos, they file their teeth, they are naked and worship various animist things. Sex is a powerful part of their lives. The men stretch their penises and their girls take great pride in the fact that they have the longest clitorises of any tribe – they say a perfect girl can have a clitoris that can grab a man's penis and hold it. They drink white lightning called *Mchozi ya Simba*, 'Tears of a Lion'. They smoke weed all the time and love nothing better than hunting and eating.

I would say they were as far as you could get from the font. But as Puck they are amusing and attractive, if you remain upwind, and they really liked Jumbo Wilson. He was a teacher and, even though they had not the slightest bit of interest in what he taught, the very fact that he was a teacher was grand. It was a well-known boast in Mueda.

'We have a white teacher in Mueda district, a huge white teacher.'

'What does he teach?'

'We are not sure, but he is like an elephant. There is no bigger teacher in Mozambique, and, we think, Tanzania. He can throw a man as far as that,' pointing at a mango tree half a dozen yards off.

In Makonde a man's strength is judged by how far he can throw another man. I would go with Jumbo to the Makonde gatherings in the forest outside Mueda. They would line up to be thrown into the bush by him. As each flailing body went cartwheeling on to the dust a sigh of admiration went up from all about, and the girls would giggle and adjust the shells around their tummies.

'Go on, you can do it! Think misery!'

The author aged eight, fourth from left in the front row

The school photograph

What sort of life was **GEORGE PERKIN**'s *prewar prep school preparing him for?*

It is the summer of 1934. I am eight years old and seated cross-legged on the ground in the front row of the annual school photograph, dressed in grey flannel shorts, open-neck shirt and blazer. I have an unruly mop of fair hair and an eager, hopeful smile. Beside me sit ten other little boys wearing polite expressions, frowns or rigid smiles. In the row behind are the staff, formally presented on chairs, and behind them, standing up, two more rows of older boys between the ages of nine and 14. If you count them all up, there is a ratio of twelve staff to 32 boys – something unimaginable by present standards.

For this is one of the more exclusive preparatory boarding schools of the 1930s, dedicated to grooming its pupils to take their places in one of the suitable professions or, at least, senior managerial positions. When the photograph was taken, I had already been at this school one year – I was sent there at the age of seven. Some of the parents of these children were stationed abroad, in India or Africa, and would appear dramatically once a year at prize-givings looking lean, tanned and leathery – one father, memorably, in puttees and sola topee. Another, a Greek father, appeared sensationally in a bowler hat, monocle, pink carnation, plus-fours and spats – a costume considered appropriate for an

English gentleman. My father, less glamorously, was a successful businessman in the paper trade, and there were other fathers also in 'trade' who held sway over empires dedicated, I recall, to bed-linen, jam, buttons and corsets.

If you look at the staff in the photograph, they are mostly men, gowned from Oxford or Cambridge, one exception being matron, who appears in a cloud of starched white, looking like the nurse in the ballet of *Romeo and Juliet*. Another is Miss Featherstone. She sits in a simple summer dress, her hands meekly folded in her lap. Miss Feather-

Tears stream down his face while the agonised boys repeat their solemn vows, dressed, significantly, in very short corduroy shorts

stone taught the piano and played the harmonium in the school chapel with tremulous white hands quivering over the keys. It was said she washed her hands several times a day in lemon juice. And we treasured the story of how she and matron had once gone on a cruise together and, passing through Port Said,

had felt so contaminated that they had thrown their clothes into the Suez Canal.

And it is Miss Featherstone who holds special memories for me, because she it was who emerged three times a year at the beginning of term from the buffet at King's Cross station dressed in a belted tweed suit and a brown-brimmed felt hat, with a rather damp-looking fox fur flung rakishly across her shoulders, to gather us up and shepherd us to school in the train. And it was Miss Featherstone who sat in the carriage with us boys while I leaned out of the window to watch my mother receding in a cloud of steam on the platform. It was at such moments that I learned, early on, not only how to suppress all feeling and emotion, but also how not to feel anything at all.

But the most significant figure in the photograph is, of course, the headmaster, seated centre. He appears earnest, impressive in his gown, with a high forehead and slightly bulging eyes. Product of a strict and narrow upper-class Victorian family, he has never married and remains firmly entrenched in bachelorhood. His 'family' are his boys to whom he is dedicated and genuinely affectionate, and over whom he exercises an imaginative, rigorous, if eccentric regime.

Scouting is high on the agenda. Lord Baden-Powell is top hero, and when his pupils reach the age of eleven, he invests them into the brotherhood, standing on the altar steps on the school chapel as if he were marrying them, tears streaming down his face, while the agonised boys repeat their solemn vows dressed, significantly, in very short corduroy shorts, a matter on which he laid particular stress. Once a year he takes a chosen few camping in North Wales, where he has a real Red Indian tepee. The programme is unorthodox, adventurous and includes strange rituals, one of which involved a performance around the camp fire at midnight in grass skirts, known as the Swazzi Wallah dance.

Of course nowadays the whole set-up might be ringed around with scepticism: all those slightly eccentric bachelors locked away in the countryside with young boys in very short shorts. Not that anything improper, so far as I know, ever took place, although the headmaster was much given to horseplay, dragging us violently around by one hand and pinching our knees hard under the dining-table until we winced. But the atmosphere was heavily monastic if not misogynistic: girls inhabited another planet, were never mentioned and never seen. The outside world never penetrated the walls of our private domain. We never saw a newspaper or heard a wireless. Social matters were never discussed. Our letters home were carefully scrutinised before the envelopes were sealed. Parents were allowed to visit for two half-Sundays a term between morning and evening chapels. All this was considered to be in the best interests of 'education' and preparation for life.

Now, in my late seventies, surveying the wreckage of my past emotional life, it would be facile to point accusing fingers: others more robust than I survived unscathed, although I know some who didn't. I wonder why, though, this period of my life should emerge as the most potent memory. I cannot altogether forget leaning out of the train window with Miss Featherstone and the boys, watching the receding figure of my mother in her blue hat and coat and pearls, waving before going off to lunch in Fortnum and Mason's from where my tuck box was generously stocked. No emotion, of course. Certainly not in front of the other boys.

Oh well, perhaps it all stood us in good stead. A few years after the photograph was taken, most of us were in the forces. I notice one particular boy in the second row of the photograph, a special friend, brilliant at the piano. He was killed in a bombing raid over Germany.

We salute you

RICHARD WALKER *reveals what really happened when the German Grand Fleet surrendered in 1919...*

As I approach my nineties people sometimes ask for my earliest memories. My maternal grandfather was born in 1817, the year Jane Austen died, but I never got a chance to question him. No doubt he could have called up talk about the Battle of Waterloo, and might even have remembered the publication of Keats's 'Ode to a Nightingale'. My other grandfather was born in 1851 and claimed he could remember soldiers returning from the Crimea.

I can't beat Compton Mackenzie. He was certain he remembered leaning out of his pram, aged one, to see a black rabbit. But I like to think my first glimpse of the past was to witness the surrender of the German Grand Fleet in 1919 at Invergordon. My father was stationed at Rosyth then, and took two of his sons, aged five and three, to see this historic event. Do I actually remember sitting on his shoulders, or is it just a vivid mental image formed from constant repetition? I'm not sure.

Certainly, in my mind is a clear picture of those huge grey shapes looming out of the North Sea mists. As they approached the pier, where a small group of British brass hats waited to receive the salute, I can see the German sailors lining the fo'c'sle heads. I can hear the shrill signal of the bo's'n's pipe. I can see the strange movements as, to a man, they lowered their trousers. I can hear the second signal a moment later as they hoisted them up again and orderly ranks were resumed. The whole operation took only a few seconds.

An oil painting, Der Tag, now in the Imperial War Museum, was painted by an Admiralty war artist, Charles Pears, and my family has a Remarque-proof colour print of it, signed by the artist and by Admiral of the Fleet, Earl Beatty. It shows no signs of German sailors on the bows, and I have never seen any reference to them in naval

In my mind is a clear picture of those huge grey shapes looming out of the North sea mists

histories. My father used to say my brother and I were the only civilians present on the pier. So presumably there were no reporters or press photographers there either. I have asked quite a number of old sea-dogs, but no one seems to have heard of it. The whole incident appears to have been hushed up – or perhaps it exists only in my imagination. Alas, my father and my brother are no longer with us to help.

He's back and he's gay

Lecherous old layabout **WILFRED DE'ATH** *insists he has tired of the company of women and has decided to swing the other way. Chaps, you have been warned...*

For some years now, I have been aware of homosexual tendencies within myself. These do not take a particularly physical form so much as a desire to spend my time with other men rather than with women. On the advice of a very old friend, John Tydeman, distinguished former head of BBC radio drama, himself gay, I have decided not to suppress these feelings but live them out.

The great thing about homosexuality is that it gets you out of the house. Having made my decision, I lost no time in speeding down to Provence to stay with a friend, Mark Jones, a medical journalist whom I have long suspected of being gay. Mark and I originally met at the Thursday Club, an English-speaking group in Avignon.

I couldn't help noticing that Mark, 44, although not specially good-looking, enjoyed phenomenal success with young French women. This was because he never, unlike the rest of us, attempted to 'hit on' them. They felt, as one attractive student explained to me, safe with him.

Mark installed me in the guest room of his comfortable house right next door to L'Eglise Orthodoxe where I worked as a *concierge non salarié* (unpaid janitor) four summers ago. Nothing actually happened during the five days I was there other than an increasing awareness of a growing bond between us, as well as a hatred, bordering in my case on paranoid misogyny, of all the women who came to call...

Things reached a climax on my last night *chez* Mark when, about to go out and eat at Pago Pago, Avignon's famous gay restaurant, we were disturbed by a self-obsessed artist named Christiane who came round in tears because her latest client had refused to pay her for a painting and the garage hadn't got her car ready, as they'd promised.

I have no intention, I hasten to add, of painting my own (rather becoming) toenails red or any other colour

Mark, who has a kind heart, made her tea and listened patiently to her woes. Personally I hated the sight of her, even though she was quite attractive. For one dreadful moment, I thought Mark was going to ask her to join us for dinner. I had to face the fact: I just wanted to be alone with Mark.

Pago Pago, where I had eaten before, was something else. It flies the multicoloured flag of international gaydom outside its doors and, when we arrived, the gay waiters descended on us like hungry wolves. (I am quite famous in Avignon.) The food was superb. Unfortunately, I had to reject the advances of the owner-manager, Frank, as a result of which I found the price of a bottle of Côtes du Rhône (€14.50) added on to my bill. Mark told me later that this was normal practice at Pago Pago for those who won't play the game. In the gay world, as in every other world, one lives and learns.

Back at the villa, I found a message from Bernard Méda on Mark's answerphone. Bernard is my oldest friend in France and I have long suspected him of being gay, too. The confirmation of this seemed to arrive with the hot weather, when Bernard, who always wears open-toed sandals, suddenly started painting his toenails a bright cherry-red. When he kissed me next day at the start of a wonderful lunch party at his beautiful country pad near Carpentras, he couldn't resist drawing my attention to them. I wish I could say this 'turned me on', but it didn't. At the same time, I must admit that I couldn't take my eyes off them. I was, as they say, riveted.

I have no intention, I hasten to add, of painting my own (rather becoming) toenails red or any other colour. Over our protracted lunch in the fine Provençal sunshine, I couldn't help being reminded of what somebody once said when I told them that I found the thought of going to bed with another man absolutely disgusting: 'Only a homosexual would say that.'

NATIONAL TREASURES

PORCELAIN FIGURINES

Available as a set for the first time! Yours for just £899.98

Britain is made Great by many things –

our 'Dunkirk spirit' in times of crisis, Morris dancing on the village green, *The Archers* at teatime – and of course those individuals who are our 'National Treasures'. Collect and keep your very own set of **National Treasures** – those indomitable men and women whose cosy, unthreatening personalities or long-past glories have made them loveable icons of Britishness.

STEPHEN FRY

This beautifully crafted Stephen Fry stands 4½ inches tall, and is a timeless replica of the comedian, actor, presenter, novelist, Renaissance man and manic depressive which will delight and entertain you for years to come.

ALAN BENNETT

Now everybody's favourite loveably dour playwright and unthreatening homosexual can adorn your mantelpiece. The expertly finished hand-colouring is definitely worth 'writing home' about!

JUDI DENCH

Lovingly handcrafted in stylish Oscarnight attire, ready to pick up another award for her stony-faced brilliance, we're sure that your Dame Judi figurine will take 'centre stage' in your collection.

SIR TREVOR MCDONALD

There was outcry when Britain's best-loved black man and News at Ten newsreader was taken from our screens. Thank goodness he's back in the 'iconic timeslot' once more. Never risk being without him again by owning this beautiful porcelain figurine.

DON'T DELAY, ORDER YOUR SET NOW! CALL 0800 123 456

with **MARY KENNY**

Henry Metelmann
German soldier

Henry Metelmann is a widower aged 80. He is a retired railway worker and lives in Godalming, Surrey, where he acts as a voluntary gardener for Charterhouse School. He was born in Hamburg and served in Hitler's Wehrmacht on the Russian front.

I was born on Christmas Day 1922. My father was an unskilled worker but I had loving parents who did their very best for me. I was an only child. My father had low wages. His cultural life was nil. They both had a great potential for education, but they never had the opportunity. Reactionary forces were very strong in Germany at this time – the aristocracy, the Churches, the German establishment. When I went into the Army all my officers were 'von'. A bloke like me would have had no chance to be an officer.

My father taught me a lot which I did not then accept. I was always arguing with him – he wanted a socialist world. He said to me, 'Do you want our globe, our earth, to be owned by certain classes? The earth belongs to all of us and it must be administered justly.' But I was a National Socialist ideologue! To me the Führer was the greatest thing.

In our part of town [Altona], our fathers were too poor to buy us a football. We played with a tennis ball. But then the Nazis came along and started sports clubs. The Hitler Youth provided us with gymnasiums, swimming pools, and you could go to camps in the summer by the mountains and the rivers.

I used to come home singing Nazi songs. I sang a song: 'When Jewish blood springs from our knives'! My parents were aghast. Everything stupid inspired me. Everyone had a copy of *Mein Kampf* and I read it diligently. My father used to say, 'You think you are pushing, but you are being pushed.' He died at the outbreak of the war. His words often come back to me.

I was apprenticed to be a locksmith, and then I got my call-up papers, in 1940. I thought it was great! Die for your Fatherland! Germany would win the war – this was the most powerful country in the world. Hitler made many speeches: we were the most intelligent and efficient nation with a cultural level higher than all the others, etc, etc. I listened, thinking, 'You're right, you're right,' without understanding anything.

I was full of myself as a German soldier in the Panzerjäger [tank regiment]. I was chosen to be a driver. Most of us were between 18 and 19; almost all had been in the Hitler Youth. Most of my comrades were ordinary decent human beings who were put into a uniform and into a position where they had to conquer and kill, or be killed.

I was transported into Russia. Then you began to see the reality of 'fight for your Fatherland'. It was a hell of our creation. You had to keep going because the alternative was to die. The coldest I remember was minus 54 degrees Centigrade. If you touched metal, your skin stuck to it, and you had to tear it off. Some did it on purpose in order to get out of the situation. If they were suspected of doing that they were shot.

I killed people. There was a wounded man – I had to drive over him. He was lying in a ditch, and I stopped the tank. It was the last thing I wanted, to drive over someone. My commander shouted, 'Why are you stopping?' and I said, 'There's someone here, he's alive,' and he ordered me to drive on. I had no

choice, but even so, that's no excuse. To save my life, I killed him.

I also killed a friend of mine. We were marching through the snow, like Napoleon's army. We were a battle group, not a regiment, just a few stragglers put together. Six of us got separated from the rest. We had no maps, no idea where we were going, but we walked one after the other through the snow towards the west. Two Russian planes turned up, as the winter sun was very low, and they fired through the snow at us. One of us was hit – Willi, a good friend of mine. He was torn open at the side. The evening before we had played chess together. None of us had any medicine. He was dying, but he

I went down on my knees and stroked his head, and with the other hand I shot the pistol into his heart

was still moaning. We stood around him, frightened and confused, and the others – who were younger – pointed to me, and I realised that it was my duty. I went down on my knees and stroked his head and said, 'Willi, it's all right, Willi, it's okay,' and with the other hand I shot the pistol into his heart. He died instantly. And then we shovelled snow over him and moved on. Had that been reported I could have been court-martialled and executed.

Soldiers were always court-martialled for refusing an order – the death sentence to be carried out within 24 hours, no appeal. A friend of mine became a lieutenant, and when it was seen that he didn't fight to the very end, in East Prussia, he was executed.

I began to see that it was all too idiotic for words and to realise that there was a possibility that Germany might lose the war. And then I fell in love with a Russian girl. Nothing happened, but I saw her as a human being. The Russians were human beings, not *Untermenschen*. I wanted to be friendly with the Russians, I wanted to learn Russian. I talked to girls – they told me that their parents were proud that they were going to university so that people could learn, could build for the future, and they asked me, 'Why do you come here to destroy all that?'

I turned 180 degrees when I understood. I am now against most war. I took part in peace marches against the dreadful war in Iraq. I am still in touch with two of my old army comrades and we all think along the same lines.

In 1945, Henry became a prisoner of the Americans, and was taken crop-picking in Arizona and Montana, and then routed back to England. He got back to Germany in 1948, though his mother was now dead.

After the war, they didn't want to talk about it in Germany. 'That was war,' they used to say –'*Das war Krieg.*' I couldn't settle down in Germany again, though, so I came back to England where I had been a prisoner of war. In 1950, I married Monika, who had been a lovely Swiss au pair girl here. We had a son in 1954 and a daughter in 1956. My dear wife died in 1980. I realise now that my father was right about so many things.

'I managed to knock him down'

EXPAT
SONALI CHAPMAN

Paris, France

CHILDHOOD FAMILY holidays in France hold uncomfortable memories of being forced to pee in dirty roadside 'toilets' in which the loos were no more than holes in the ground. Years on, Parisian loos remain terrifying: more often than not the toilet will be a hole in the ground with foot pads either side, the whole thing – ceiling, floor, walls and door – being made entirely out of stainless steel, apparently for ease of cleaning, though the permanently flooded floors and damp trouser bottoms on exiting do not inspire one with confidence. But when it comes to the cleanliness of their swimming pools, Parisians are fastidious.

My boyfriend and I discovered this during a trip to our local public pool. I was wearing an ordinary swimsuit and he was in swimming shorts – very sensible, to-the-knee swimming trunks, not the loud 'Bermuda shorts' kind: our usual swimming attire that passes muster in London. We strutted confidently poolside, only semi-conscious of the tut-tutting of our fellow-swimmers. Suddenly, just as we were about to dive in, a voice boomed out: 'Arrêtez-vous!'
We stopped immediately, fearing towel-theft or some such. Looking around, I saw a dozen or so people staring right back at me, and it dawned on me that the 'Stop!' was directed at us.

A svelte but smug lifeguard made his way over and began to speak French at break-neck speed. His angry gesticulating seemed to point to my hair and my boyfriend's general demeanour. 'Excusez-moi,' I ventured. 'Nous sommes anglais, pouvez-vous parler plus lentement s'il vous plaît?' The lifeguard broke into a smug smile and gave a little chuckle. 'Ah, yes, zee English. C'est clair.'

Visions of Inspector Clouseau filled my head, but my boyfriend, unphased, continued: 'Il y a un problème, monsieur?'

'Yes, zhere is. Trousers not allowed.'

'Trousers?'

'Yes. Not allowed. You wear zee trousers.'

'These are my swimming trunks.'

The lifeguard chuckled knowingly. 'Zey are not allowed in France. In France we wear correct swimming clothes. Zey are too long, too wide. Your English pools must be very dirty. It is not hygienic.' He was getting into the swing of things now. 'And you, mademoiselle. Your head.'

'What's wrong with my head?'

'No hat. You must wear hat in the pool. Your hair is... big.'

A few swimmers nearby, in caps, giggled self-assuredly. Smug lifeguard looked serious. 'You can buy zeez things from the machine. But you cannot swim in zis pool looking like zis.'

Overwhelmed with embarrassment and feeling incredibly exposed, I couldn't think of a single witty riposte. Instead, the two of us were shamed out of the swimming pool and back to the changing rooms. 'I'm not bloody swimming here again. How dare he be so rude?' I said, filling with anger. 'He's just French,' my boyfriend replied, ever reasonable. 'We've come all the way here. And anyway, I could do with a new pair of trunks. I'll meet you back here.'

A few minutes later, I was donning my newly purchased swimming cap. My boyfriend appeared sheepishly. I couldn't help it; I began to giggle. He was wearing the smallest, tightest pair of Speedo swimming trunks I had ever seen.
He looked like an extra from a Seventies Miami Vice episode – only more bereft.

'This is the only pair they sell. I can't believe they've made me wear this.'

'They look fine,' I lied. 'Let's just get this over with.'

'There's no dignity anymore,' he mumbled.

Back at the edge of the pool, smug lifeguard burst out laughing and began to clap. 'Bravo, bravo!' There were sniggers from the swimmers. 'Et voilà,' he continued. 'Ze petit anglais has become français!'

'I'm afraid we're going to have to let you go.'

The world according to
Enfield Snr

Confessions of a common criminal

I read in the paper that the members of some group or other are complaining that we people with dogs are disturbing the wildlife. Ramblers, they call us, which I suppose is one degree less offensive than hikers, and they say that we ought to keep our dogs under better control. Some ponderous spokesman for this association says that it is an offence at law to disturb the wildlife with a dog, and I am not a bit surprised, as most things are illegal these days. No doubt to let a spaniel chase a pigeon is the sort of criminal act that would land you in front of the magistrates if a bobby caught you at it.

As far as our dog is concerned, she being a greyhound, disturbing the wildlife is one of her principal pleasures. In fact, I think she likes it better than anything else, even more than eating, though perhaps slightly less than being made a fuss of. She disturbs the rabbits all the time, although she never catches one, as they are unsporting creatures and do not run into the middle of the field for a game of tag, but dive down their holes, leaving her bouncing about outside. She disturbs pheasants occasionally, putting them to the frightful inconvenience of flying away. She is in two minds about disturbing swans. If she sees them in the water meadows she advances towards them in a purposeful manner, and if they take to the air she rushes along underneath them in a way they may find disturbing, but if they stand their ground she thinks better of it and lets them alone. That is all she is guilty of so far.

If I am ever prosecuted for allowing these fearful offences I shall argue that she is not nearly as disturbing to wildlife as wildlife itself. Burns's 'inhumanity' of man to man is not as bad as the bestiality of beast to beast. Lottie, that being her name, is not nearly as disturbing to the rabbits as are the foxes, stoats and weasels which prey upon them all the time. Having lost that argument (for common sense rarely prevails in such cases), I will plead in mitigation that she conveys great benefit to the wildlife in other ways by thoroughly disturbing any cats that may come into our garden. I can fairly describe our garden as a cat-free zone, to the great advantage of small birds and fieldmice, which are only at risk from other wildlife, such as the sparrowhawk which pounces upon them from time to time.

Another doubtful activity that I go in for is picking primroses. The law forbids the picking of certain wildflowers, and

All this wildlife legislation has made me nervous, and if I am walking along with a bunch of primroses in my hand I tend to hide it under my coat

whether this includes primroses I know not, but I pick them anyway as a bunch of primroses in spring is a lovely sight, and they smell nice. If not illegal in itself, it may be theft. Most of those I pick are our own primroses as we have a little paddock where they grow, but I also take them from the verges by the road so I may be stealing local authority primroses. We have lived in our house since 1960, picking primroses in 47 consecutive springs, and they are just as plentiful as ever. It is hard to imagine anything less harmful to the world at large, but all this wildlife legislation has made me nervous, and if I am walking along with a bunch of primroses in my hand I tend to hide it under my coat.

Many years ago I was talking to Dr David Hessayon, the great gardening expert, and rather officiously told him that making bonfires is supposed to be a dangerous practice as there are said to be more carcinogens in a whiff of bonfire smoke than in ever so many cigarettes. 'Mr Enfield,' he said, 'you have just destroyed the last innocent pleasure of my life.' I have started to feel like that about exercising Lottie and picking primroses, which I fear I now do in a sly and furtive manner, in the hope of escaping notice. If I am seen in a field blatantly picking flowers while the greyhound disturbs the wildlife, someone will probably inform on me and then I shall feel the heavy hand of the law upon my collar. And yet, in my boyhood, there could be no more innocent pastimes than walking a dog or picking wild flowers.

'Slow down, mind that rock, keep off the rough road...'

Goodbye, Pet

A hole in the garden is no longer good enough for our dear departed furry friends,
says **DAEMIENNE SHEEHAN**

The funeral director was a hesitant man in old brown shoes worn down at the heels and a faded jumper. Just over his shoulder I could see a fresh plot covered in flowers and, beyond that, a tractor trawling the fields. 'He was ten stone,' the director said with awe, 'with a head like this.' He stretched his hands out like a fisherman describing the one that got away. I gasped. 'I had no idea bloodhounds were so large,' I said. 'Oh yes,' he nodded solemnly. 'It was my first bloodhound. Ugly but quite extraordinary. A young couple owned him. He had stomach problems, I believe. We buried him on a Friday.' I asked whether they ever buried smaller pets. 'Well,' he said thoughtfully, 'we do get quite a lot

of iguanas. Usually very young. They're not suited to this country, you know. It only makes them miserable. It's a bit like having a dolphin for a pet, really.'

Surrey Pet Cemetery in Godstone is a husband-and-wife operation, although the Johnsons also have a partner, an ex-snail farmer. 'This office was once filled with snails,' Mr Johnson smiled mildly. Now the walls are plastered with Polaroids of departed pets, while above

Oddly adorable, the tiny plots in the toy-sized cemetery are marked by ceramic animals

the director's desk is a drawing of a cherry tree in blossom. In fact, the blossoms turn out to be paper squares representing 300 plots. Between 700 and 800 animals a month are cremated at the cemetery. Of these, Mr Johnson explains, 200 are special cremations, with the ashes returned to the owners in a complimentary scatter box or miniature casket. Then there are the burials with an optional CD recording of the service and a visit to the chapel. The only difficulty Mr Johnson seems to have is finding a priest to perform funeral rites. It's a question of having the right sort of soul. Animals, according to the Church of England, are not endowed with the same souls as humans and therefore cannot be given the same funeral rites.

*'I plan to be filthy rich.
I'm halfway there already'*

Fortunately, Mr Johnson has the services of an ex-C of E minister who considers himself a Christian first and a denomination second.

But the nicest ceremony Mr Johnson witnessed was non-denominational – the funeral of Red Rory. Red Rory had been cherished by a black South London family and a dozen people came down to officiate at his funeral. Forming a devotional ring around the grave, each person took it in turns to relate a story about the family dog.

The saddest funeral Mr Johnson saw was for a dog owned by a lad from a Peckham council estate. The boy broke down completely, surprising even unshockable Mr Johnson. 'I later found out that the dog was the closest friend he had. They spent day and night together and he didn't know how he would get by without him.'

Oddly adorable, the tiny plots in the toy-sized cemetery are marked by ceramic animals, and the only sounds to be heard for miles are of livestock, tractors and wild birds. With the proviso that both parties are cremated, owners may also be buried with their faithful friends when their time comes. It's a long way from how dead pets used to be treated. Forty years ago, a cemetery was started in Cambridge by an ex-rubbish collector who was tired of coming across dead pets laid to rest on the bins. Now there's an Association of British Private Pet Cemeteries and Crematoria and international get-togethers with the Americans who take a bigger approach. Cemeteries across the water are the size of shopping malls, while the Dutch win the sensitivity awareness sweepstakes again: in Holland, vets refer bereaved owners to pet cemeteries.

Mr Johnson says that he likes the Americans. 'They're terribly well organ-ised and such nice people. Most people in this business are. I always say our customers are generally more caring than the average person. We have one gay couple who insist on cleaning up afterwards. They wash up everything and put it back in place.'

Still, it's hard to take the business seriously with names like Paws to Close, Happy Hunting, Mutts Cuts and Pets Royale. Do people mock Mr Johnson when they find out about this job? He nodded wisely. 'Oh, they all think it's rather amusing, but then they're usually the ones who have never had a pet.' He paused as the strip lighting flickered overhead. A poster behind him showed a row of Dalmatians waiting at a fire hydrant. 'In this world,' he said quietly, I don't think many people realise what the loss of a pet can do. One poor woman lost her dog and it was all she had in the world. She's 85. When you're that age, you're unlikely to outlive your pet, but she was devastated.'

A cemetery was started forty years ago by an ex-rubbish collector who was tired of finding dead pets in the bins

Many of the owners sign themselves Mummy or Daddy in the Remembrance Book at Surrey Cemetery. 'He touched everyone's heart with a special love,' reads one. 'A little poodle with a lion's heart, the love for him will never lessen. Love Mummy and Daddy.' 'Well,' says Mr Johnson. 'they never stop needing you in the same way as children, so perhaps it is right to use those terms.'

Foster-parents might be more accurate. So many of the pets buried at Surrey stumbled into their new homes broken, battered or even scarred by cigarettes. Or perhaps they were merely accident-prone. There was one colossally clumsy pigeon. When discovered in the street by a family of good Samaritans, the pigeon had already lost his left eye. Unfortunately, the family also owned a cat. As the pigeon entered the house for the first time, the cat leapt up and gave chase, one-eyed, the pigeon flew into a wall and broke its wing. Months passed. The unlucky pigeon recovered and was released into the wild. The family wondered whether they had taken the right decision – was he too spatially unaware to cope? How would he get by with one eye? They returned home to a familiar cooing. It came from the upstairs room, where their invalid mother lay in bed. The pigeon had made up his own mind. For the remaining years of his life he stayed in the mother's room while the cat stayed downstairs.

Back in South London, there was the case of the fairground owner of no fixed address who lost his dog. Months later, he was visiting new friends on an estate. From across a corridor he heard a familiar bark. 'Don't go there,' his friends warned him. 'Your dog's been taken by junkies.' But the owner decided to risk it. The inhabitants were indeed addicts, and also animal-lovers. They returned the dog along with all the food they bought for him.

Mr Johnson beams when I point out the unnaturally high level of bad luck these animals initially have. 'Yes,' he says. 'It's as if we're saying. "Well, no one else loved you but we do. We think you're wonderful." And they really are.'

IT'S YOUR SHOUT, BILL

AAAAGGGHHH!

Who's this guy Fawkes?

Alec Guinness December 2005

EW Swanton December 2004

Tony Benn December 2002

Wally Fawkes, the veteran political cartoonist Trog, drew caricatures for *The Oldie*'s Book Review pages every month from 2001 to 2005 (see over). Now 84, Fawkes retired three years ago after sixty-odd years as a cartoonist as failing eyesight meant he could no longer see well enough to draw.

He spoke to Margaret Crick in an interview for *The Oldie* in 2007:

'Fawkes thinks good cartoonists need highly trained graphic skills and political awareness, but he doesn't believe in taking work too

seriously. "It's just part of the paper which is fish and chips the next day." Nevertheless, his originals are sought after by many politicians, including the jazz-loving Ken Clarke [Fawkes is also a keen jazz musician], who says Trog is his favourite political cartoonist.'

Trog's 'own leanings are to the left. "I'm all for the left being sensible, or at least regaining its senses. I like New Labour but not Tony Blair. I've done lots of cartoons of Blair, week after week, and think that's what drove me blind."'

Queen Victoria October 2002

Max Hastings January 2003

Robert Baden-Powel May 2004

Max Beerbohm April 2003

Colin Dexter March 2003

Janet Street-Porter August 2004

Graham Greene and Yvonne Cloetta July 2004

One night in Biarritz

... is enough for a lifetime. **ROBIN DALTON** *on encountering an old schoolfriend whose cataracts, food fetishism and very particular sleeping habits shook her Atlantic haven*

W e were not 'best friends' at school but part of a close-knit group. We were expelled together for diving, naked except for voluminous heavy brown gabardine school capes, into the swimming pool of the grand country hotel where our parents were allowed to take us for lunch on 'visiting weekends'. Our names were read out at assembly next morning. My father talked the headmistress into giving us a second chance.

Until a chance encounter, we had not met for 60 years. Biarritz, I told her, was my lifeline. I had had a second home there for 30 years; a paradise for ocean addicts, it was our birthplace of Australia transported into Europe. She decided that she would sell her Kensington apartment and move to Biarritz, the alternative being a lonely London life or a return to Australia. I remembered that at school she was tremendously organised, forever making 'lists', and was not too surprised by her swift decision, reached after an intensive quiz as to a) the climate of Biarritz, b) its cultural opportunities and c), most important, its medical facilities and the excellence of its eye surgeons. She had glaucoma, macular degeneration and a cataract, and mistrusted British surgeons. I was asked to make an appointment for her cataract operation during the week she would be there.

M ore telephone calls booked her on the flight with me, and a room at a small *auberge*: wonderful food, charming *patron* and *patronne*, certain to be clean and comfortable, if basic, and at a terrific rate. We met on the coach to the airport, she armed with her plastic travelling bucket. It was never unpacked, she told me, and contained her entire supply of cosmetics, toilet articles, medicines, emergency rations, water, thermos of coffee, compass, torch, several maps, pencils, notebooks, eye masks, glasses, plastic

knives, forks, spoons. In her flight bag were carefully wrapped (and delicious) sandwiches, chocolate biscuits and an apple. She did not approve of airport or aeroplane food, or coffee.

T he flight was trouble-free. We were shown her room in the *auberge*. It was minute but spotless, with a small but adequate shower room.

'Oh,' said M. 'May I have a room with a smaller bed?' Nobody in France ever asks for a smaller bed, and Madame la Patronne said there were none. M claimed that she was unable to sleep in a double bed. I left her, to meet in an hour or so for dinner.

Later, M la P told me my friend had changed rooms. I found her stripping and remaking the bed (still 4 ft 6 in) in another minute, identical room, but at the back of the hotel, facing a brick wall instead of a pleasant street. Streets have motor cars, and it might be noisy, but the bed-making? 'Look,' she said. 'The window gives its air to the foot of the bed: I must have it on my face. I will sleep at this end. And no underblanket. I cannot possibly sleep without an underblanket, so I have put the blanket provided underneath and now – help me – I am making the coverlet into a duvet.' She was, too. I was given one end and we folded together. As she must have been nearly blind (glaucoma, MD *and* cataract), I pointed out that the bed light was now at her feet and that the room was rather dark with no other lighting. No matter... I left her to her duvet-making and went downstairs for a large drink.

We ate an excellent dinner – except that the menu in her demi-pension was beef and she wouldn't eat beef, so Madame graciously provided salmon. I was to tell Madame that she wanted to make her own bed every day. She disliked being tucked in.

I had come to Biarritz to supervise building work on my new house, and she had assured me of her independence. However, I felt I must devote our first day to her, so I went to fetch her at 10 am. I thought our local market might enchant her, but she was not impressed. At Véronique's she fingered every fruit and vegetable before announcing that she would like to buy some watercress. Véronique produced a magnificent bunch, pretty enough to place in a vase, tied it in a bag and handed it over. 'May I see it, please?' Véronique had to untie the bag and hold it aloft. 'Oh no, that is far too large: may I have a smaller one?' The watercress went back with its fellows.

After a spartan lunch she declared she had to sleep for an hour after lunch each day – it seems she had a leaking heart valve. There was one bed in my borrowed apartment, but there was still a bed upstairs in the grand apartment I had just sold. We took a pillow and blanket upstairs, where I struggled with the shutters to give her some air. Later, she did not want to walk in the hilly town, so I drove her to our splendid beach. She was not really interested and it was, in any case, grey and damp. Biarritz had let me down. I had extolled its beauty when the sun shone. About the hills, which left her out of breath, I

could do nothing. She wanted to see St Jean de Luz, Bayonne and some of the adjoining villages, all hilly. We wandered aimlessly until it was time to take her back to the hotel. We arranged that I would collect her at 10 am for a possible excursion to Bayonne. I went home and got quietly drunk.

I arrived punctually to find her in the lobby, seated, hatted and coated, with suitcase by her side. I assumed

I found her in the lobby, seated, hatted and coated, with suitcase by her side. 'It's not the hotel – it's the place. It's a hell-hole'

some disaster had occurred in the night and apologised profusely for choosing an unsuitable hotel. 'It's not the hotel, it's the place – it's a hell-hole. I will go home today.' This involved an hour on the hotel telephone. I had to cancel the appointment with the eye surgeon, and find out from Ryanair if there was a seat on the plane that evening. Christine, my friend at Ryanair, said it would cost an extra £170 to change the cheap ticket I had been so proud of getting for her. She wavered: Christine and I hung on. She decided to leave it until the last moment

as she had much experience of arguing at airports: she would turn up at the last minute, pleading a weak heart, and they would take her for nothing, providing I kept my distance and left it to her.

At the airport I was ordered to look after the bucket and keep it out of sight. I waited in the background as M argued with Christine, clasping her heart and panting. After 15 minutes of watching Christine's patient but exasperated face, I intervened and told her it was not Christine's own airline. But Christine had an idea. 'Madame, if you wish to go tomorrow rather than today, it will cost you £27 less.' M thought this might be the solution. Remembering the rug, the pillow, the shutters, the tiny shared bathroom, I quickly pointed out that the strain of unpacking, wasting the carefully prepared sandwiches and thermos, might prove too much for her heart – and for only £27? I pushed her and her bucket to the check-in counter, and ran.

The following night she rang from a hospital in London. They had taken her blood pressure and pulse rate – 120, she told me. Nobody had thought of taking mine.

'Welcome to Mensa. If you know the extension number of the person you wish to reach, multiply it by your height in centimetres'

How's your father?

ANTHONY PERRY's *father left home in a newly purchased Lagonda car with a blonde lady when he was still a baby. Years later their paths crossed in a peculiar way...*

In 1963 or thereabouts, while still a youngish man hoping for elusive fame or at least fortune, I found myself attending the consulting rooms of one Dr Wilfred Bion at 135 Harley Street. I went each day for 50 minutes of beneficial psychoanalysis and an opportunity to whinge about how unfair life had been to me. I lay each day on his leatherette slab delving into my past, muttering imprecations against all those who had failed to love me and in particular, of course, my mother, who had clearly not wanted me and barely cared whether I lived or died. It was an expensive way of getting one's own back.

My father, Raymond, whom I had hardly known, came in for his share of abuse. He had left home in a newly purchased Lagonda car with a blonde lady while I was still a baby – on the advice of a psychiatrist, so my mother claimed, who had told him that a little of what he fancied would do him good. Such advice we should all get, and I never saw him again or heard from him until I was 19.

I phoned him up when I came out of the army. 'Hello, old boy,' he said, as if we had parted the week before, and suggested we meet for dinner at the Café Royal. 'You'll recognise me, I'm as bald as a coot.'

We were friends for a couple of years and then we had a serious row over the ownership of my grandfather's ivory-topped swagger stick (dig that, Dr Freud!), after which he moved away to the country and I lost track of him again.

So each day I lay, consorting with my new father, pouring out my woes and trying to shift the blame for my delinquent and unfulfilled life onto my unloving parents.

But something rather surprising was to happen. After one particularly satisfying session I came bounding down the stairs, full of useful 'in-sights', stumbled, picked myself up and leant against the hall table for a moment.

There, on the table, was a letter addressed to me. 'A. R. Perry', it said.

I am Richard Anthony, so sometimes people put 'A. R.', but something rum-

> ## Was it really possible that, as I lay on Dr Bion's couch, just above me had been the soles of my father's shoes, with his feet inside them?

bled in my head. I went down to the receptionist. 'Is this letter for me?' I asked.

'No, it's for the gentleman in the flat upstairs.'

I hadn't seen my father for years but my brother had once given me a HUNter telephone number for him – the relief exchange then covering Baker Street and Harley Street. My mind spun. Could it possibly be...?

Then, 'Would Mr Perry perhaps be a bald-headed man, about sixty?' I asked. 'A Mr Arthur Raymond Perry?'

'Yes,' she said brightly. 'Do you know him? He's just moved. I've promised to send on his letters.'

Was it really possible that, as I lay recumbent on Père Bion's couch, staring up at the ceiling, just above me had been the soles of my father's shoes, with his feet inside them? If you don't believe me or fail to regard this as wholly extraordinary, stop reading now and get on with your miserable, unanalysed and entirely predictable lives.

And it really was true, and I remember hugging the news to myself – barely able to wait to report to the stern and impenetrable Dr Bion. He would be surprised. Perhaps he would begin future lectures: 'I once had an interesting patient [me] whose uncaring father...' And the psychoanalytical world would come to a numbed halt at the amazing situation when it was written up in the medical journals.

Alas, it was not to be. The moment I arrived at the next day's session I blurted out my story. There was a long silence. Bion seldom rushed into print but there was a longer silence than usual.

'What,' he eventually asked, 'what significance do you attach to this coincidence?'

And there was none. It was just that, a coincidence, albeit an extraordinary one. Maybe he knew, or had wondered as I talked about my parents, whether the Perry upstairs was my father. He was incredibly smart and knew almost everything so he probably knew that too.

I learnt later that he was quite a big name in the analysis business, but I developed feelings of gratitude and affection for him as a human being. When he died in 1979 I was upset and felt that I had lost a father – far more so than when my own father died a few years later.

...HELLO, THIS IS
LYNSEY. HOW CAN
I HELP?

EMILO.

Jolly Barbirolli

The late Evelyn Barbirolli, oboeist and widow of conductor John Barbirolli, talked to **RICHARD INGRAMS** *at the 2002 Oldie Piano Weekend in Cambridge*

I never met him again, so it was a very special pleasure to welcome his widow Evelyn to the 2002 Oldie Piano Weekend at Magdalene College, Cambridge. Her maiden name of Evelyn Rothwell will be familiar to all oldie music lovers, I myself having been brought up on the famous Adolf Busch recordings of the Brandenburg Concertos in which she played first oboe to Busch's first violin. Those recordings were made as long ago as 1935. But there was nothing of the ancient relic about the lady who joined us in the Magdalene College bar on the evening of 5 April 2002 and was soon chatting animatedly to the participating pianists over a scotch and water.

Although she had given up playing about 20 years earlier, unable any longer to make the tongue movements that the oboe demands, Evelyn was still active in the musical world, mainly as an adjudicator in competitions. Apart from music, her main interest was in her garden, an interest she had perhaps inherited from her father, a tea dealer who lived with his wife and three children at the village of Cholsey near Wallingford-on-Thames in Oxfordshire.

Neither of her parents was musical, although she recalled that when the members of her mother's large family got together to sing Christmas carols they were all somehow able to sing in harmony. When I asked her how she become involved with the oboe she said with typical modesty, 'Oh, by accident.' And when she won a scholarship from Downe House School to the Royal College of Music it was 'by luck'. Though when you know that at the time she had only been playing the instrument for six months, you realise what an extraordinary talent she must have had even at that early stage.

It was certainly extraordinary enough to get her a job in an orchestra and also to catch the ear (as well as the eye) of the young conductor John Barbirolli.

They were married in 1939, and by that stage she had already played in the very first performances at Glyndebourne. 'The whole thing was started for

In the summer of 1959, on holiday from Oxford, I was helping out behind the scenes at the King's Lynn Festival. The festival was organised by two quite grand ladies, both of them royal ladies-in-waiting, Lady Ruth Fermoy (later well-known as the grandmother of Princess Diana) and Lady Margaret Douglas-Home, a first cousin of my mother's. Both of them were excellent pianists and Lady Fermoy, who had studied with Cortot, was of a professional standard.

My main memory of that happy time, apart from the frightening experience of having to turn-over for Gerald Moore, was that of meeting John Barbirolli. Barbirolli conducted regularly at the Festival and also performed as a cellist with Ruth Fermoy in a chamber music concert. That year they played César Franck's Piano Quintet and I can remember watching Barbirolli playing his cello at rehearsal with a fag dangling from his mouth. He also conducted a concert of Strauss waltzes with the Pro

Arte orchestra in the Corn Exchange – I sat in on the rehearsal and witnessed Barbirolli, who rightly regarded the waltzes as great music, shouting at the orchestra, who were a bit snooty about it, 'Don't play

When I asked Evelyn Barbirolli how she became involved with the oboe she said with typical modesty, 'Oh, by accident'

it so begrudgingly!' He won them round, of course, and by the evening they were playing it with gusto.

Afterwards we all had dinner in his hotel, and when he went upstairs he told me that he used to take the score of *Meistersinger* to bed with him but nowadays he took the *Matthew Passion*. Did I think it was an improvement? I said it definitely was.

Audrey, John Christie's wife,' she said. 'She was a lovely artist but she wasn't a great singer because her voice was very small. But she sang very charmingly and had a lot of personality on stage. She was a charming Susanna and a lovely Zerlina.'

It was the musical director at Glyndebourne, Fritz Busch, who recommended Evelyn to his violinist brother, Adolf, who was then recruiting English musicians for his Brandenburg recordings. I asked her what made them so special. 'I think it was Adolf's personality – very warm, very caring. We all adored him. I was lucky enough to be his first oboe player.' (Again, she attributed her success to luck rather than her own musicianship.)

Barbirolli had meanwhile been appointed to conduct the New York Philharmonic, and Evelyn sailed to join him in October 1939, just after the outbreak of the war. On her first day at sea she met Rachmaninov and his daughter and the great composer recognised her and invited her to join him at the Captain's tea party. 'It was a very proud moment,' she remembers, speaking of Rachmaninov with great affection. 'We were very fond of him. He was a very reserved man and I think we saw a side of him that perhaps others didn't see. Of course he was a wonderful pianist. He could produce a legato like nobody else I've ever heard. He had huge hands – I think he could stretch an octave and a half. And that enormous stretch enabled him to get about and get the most beautiful sound on the piano. I knew he was always sad because he wanted to be regarded as a great composer and America at that time regarded him as a great pianist. I don't think they thought of him as a composer. He was a most gloomy-looking man. He used to smoke these Russian cigarettes which he would cut into three.'

She described going to Rachmaninov's funeral in 1943. 'It was the California summer and very hot. But we thought we ought to go. It was in a tiny Russian Orthodox church. No seats. We just stood, holding candles. And Rachmaninov was laid out in his coffin in full evening dress with one hand dangling out with a great big ring on it. There was a queue of people waiting to kiss the ring but I'm afraid we didn't. John said afterwards to the writer Michael Kennedy, "The old boy looked a lot more cheerful that he ever did on the platform."'

There was a lot of laughter at this, as

there was throughout our interview – all suggesting a very unaffected and English approach to music, but one that has perhaps been lost in the hyperprofessional world of today.

Perhaps the loudest laughter came when Evelyn told of the struggles she

Rachmaninov was laid out in his coffin. Barbirolli said, 'The old boy looked a lot more cheerful than he ever did on the platform'

and her husband had when forming the Hallé orchestra during the war following their return to England in 1943. 'We were just dying to get back.' (She told how they changed places on a plane with the actor Leslie Howard who wanted to get to England for a film première but whose plane was shot down by the Germans.)

Opposite: Lady Barbirolli signing books at the Oldie Piano Weekend. Above: John and Evelyn Barbirolli in New York, 1939. Below: Rachmaninov – 'a most gloomy-looking man'

'John held auditions for the Hallé all day and every day. No one was refused. He would hear *everybody*.' The double bass section was a special problem. One man played the scherzo of Beethoven's Fifth Symphony with tremendous vitality but he never moved his left hand, so it was all one note. Another struggled to play the double bass solo from Verdi's *Otello*, which involves the high register, and in the end Barbirolli had to show him how to do it. The old boy watched in amazement, 'I've never been oop there before!' he said finally.

As I had witnessed with the Pro Arte orchestra at King's Lynn, John Barbirolli had a knack of creating an almost instant rapport with the various orchestras he conducted. How did he do it?

'It's very hard to explain,' she said. 'I suppose it's just a case of personality.'

Later Raymond Banning asked her why it was that today's musical scene lacked the great characters, those musicians she knew and played with – Horowitz, Casals, Rubinstein. But she couldn't really explain it, except by saying that there were so many very gifted players working today that it was more difficult than it had been in her day for someone to stand out.

Afterwards the indefatigable Evelyn spent half an hour signing her book before going off to visit friends in Cambridge who wanted her advice on their garden. When I told everyone after she had gone that she was 92 there was general incredulity.

I've signed the Official Secrets Act. More than the one time you might think would suffice. And I sometimes come across other people who've done the same. There's an affinity among us that must exist between Catholics or Masons. My friend Gina, for instance. For a long time I knew her as a mother of three, a breaker of rules (a no trespassing sign is like a magnet to Gina) and a talented artist. Actually, there lies the clue. One day she let slip that she used to work for MI6, forging passports. So I felt bound to reciprocate with the information that, when I was a fresh young graduate I didn't go into teaching or nursing or Marks & Spencers. I went to work for GCHQ in Cheltenham and became a sort of electronic spy.

Gina and I felt liberated by this exchange, as if a great burden had been lifted from us in the confessional. Paradoxically we also felt naughty, telling tales out of school. For Gina this was the one rule that she hadn't broken before. And yet, disappointingly for the reader, despite my many signings of the Act, I can reveal nothing now that has not at some time since then, either accidentally or by design, entered the public domain.

The pathway to working at GCHQ was a tortuous one. I applied, passed an initial examination and was given an interview, during which I was asked if I knew the connection between Mata Hari and daisies. Anyone who knows a little Malay is likely to know that *mata hari* means sun, and I suppose they were checking that I really had spent four years at school in Malaysia, as my CV said. Possibly they were also subtly looking for signs of obsession with spying and crossword puzzles. They said that, even though I hadn't actually known that Mata Hari's code name was Daisy, they would love to have me on board, but would have to do the routine security checks, which should take a couple of months. They actually took a year, during which time I got married and got another job.

At one point during that year they asked if they could interview me a second time at my parents' home in Northamptonshire.

My life as a spy

GILLIAN CLARIDGE *has decided to spill the beans about what really went on behind the scenes during her time at GCHQ. Worried about national security? Read on...*

It was easy enough to wave a piece of card, or, for the men, to flash a tie at both checkpoints to be let in

I awaited the arrival of 'an officer from GCHQ' with some trepidation, which was justified by the sight of a huge man with thick black policeman's boots striding up the garden path. I found out later that most of the security officers at GCHQ were retired policemen. He asked me all the questions I had answered in the last interview, apart from Mata Hari. Then he said: 'Now, can you tell me how I can get back to Cheltenham from here?'

'But... haven't you just come from Cheltenham?' I asked.

'It's different going back,' he said. I see now that I was once again the subject of the very discreet inquisitorial techniques used to filter out the suspect from the merely dubious. HMG spent vast amounts of money doing checks like these, with varying degrees of success. They may be using them even now in Iraq.

I had almost given up hope of ever working for Her Majesty's Government when they offered me a job as an assistant linguist specialist. They apologised for the delay, which they said had been caused by following my tracks, not only across eastern Europe, but also to the Far East. Judging by the difficulties they appeared to have had getting from Cheltenham to Northampton and back, this must have presented considerable problems.

So I signed the Act for the second time (the first having been when I worked for the then DHSS in the university holidays) and went to work at GCHQ Oakley. I found that it was easy to keep mum in Cheltenham. Nearly everybody either worked for GCHQ or was connected to someone who did. There was no one to ask awkward questions because they all seemed to know the answers. This was in spite of the fact that the scope of the Act was vast. You might

have thought that listening posts and names of agents would be the only kind of covert material covered. Actually, even the fact that the lavatory paper inside the GCHQ complexes was imprinted with 'OHMS' was an official secret.

We were therefore careful not to reveal the sanitary arrangements at work, but this didn't prevent one or two gaps in the security. In order to enter the Oakley site we had to show our passes, usually worn on metallic cords round our necks, and meant to be concealed off the premises. If one inadvertently left the pass at home it was easy enough to wave a piece of card, or, for the men, to flash a tie at both checkpoints to be let in. There was an occasion when some Irish people on the way to the Cheltenham races were allowed to enter by showing their race cards. They were only stopped when they enquired where the horses were.

This was in the infancy of electronic security, and at one time the residents of Harp Hill, a desirable piece of real estate situated above Oakley, started to complain that curious symbols were appearing on their television sets. It turned out that these were signals that had somehow been transmitted by GCHQ computers. No one was quite sure how many Soviet spies had homes on Harp Hill, but there must have been a drop in the price of houses when they all decided to sell up.

Even the most careful screening of personnel has its limitations, and while I was there GCHQ produced a mole. Three of us worked for this gentleman for a few months. If anyone had asked us we could have told them that there might be something strange about him, but GCHQ had its share of eccentrics, and he was accepted as one. He was apparently rather deaf, which might have made him an odd choice for a transcriber of Russian conversations. But it seemed that his hearing impairment was not allowed to interfere with his work.

His name was Geoff, so we used, affectionately, to call him Mutton. He drove a smart new Volkswagen Golf which we reckoned was a little beyond the reach of someone on his salary. He wore sharp suits in terrible colours. It emerged that he was colour-blind as well as deaf. He was not a sociable person. His preferred entertainment, he told us, was films. He used to go regularly to the National Film Theatre and spent whole weekends on orgies of Ingmar Bergman or Tarkovsky.

Then there were his work hours.

Flexitime had just been introduced and it was summer. Most of us liked to start work early in the morning and finish as near to 4 pm as we could. Geoff always came in late and left late. Consequently he had the office to himself for at least two hours every day. In hindsight he was an obvious candidate for espionage, but no one cottoned on to him until several years later, when he was arrested for child molesting and I believe he confessed to removing documents from our office and passing them to his Soviet contact at the cinema. I cannot now even remember what the documents might have contained. He was sentenced to twenty years in Gloucester gaol.

So was all the security worthwhile, you may ask? The rationale of GCHQ, as for NSA in Maryland, was and still is, I suppose, the defence of the Western world. It's fine to spy on other nations if they are a potential threat to your own security. After all, they do it to you. It's even fine, apparently, to spy on the UN. The funny thing is that, having set up a hugely elaborate network of espionage in one form or another, governments do not always accept the evidence it provides. My abiding memory of my time at GCHQ is of coming home one day for lunch and being greeted by my husband, a fish farmer, saying, 'Well, you've probably known about this for weeks.' 'About what?' I asked, guardedly.

'Don't be coy… you must know. Afghanistan!'
'What about Afghanistan?' I said, thinking I must have had a premature senior moment. 'The Russians have invaded Afghanistan.' He looked at me in amazement. 'You didn't know, did you?'

No, I didn't. The need-to-know ethic had precluded an overview of the situation for all but the highest in the chain. We had known about troop movements for some time but somewhere in the upper echelons of government analysts a decision had been made that they amounted to nothing more than an exercise. The BBC news had apparently pre-empted the intelligence services.

Thirty years on, electronic surveillance must have progressed beyond my wildest imaginings. You wouldn't be able to get into GCHQ by waving your tie nowadays. The difficulty these days seems to be finding something to reveal – WMDs, for instance. It makes you wonder whether signing the Official Secrets Act has any value at all, apart from the thrill for me and Gina of spilling some already spilt beans after years of keeping mum.

'To be honest, I'm more of an agnostic myself'

Matchless Bewick

IAIN BAIN *celebrates the life and work of the radical thinker, naturalist and master wood engraver, Thomas Bewick, born over 250 years ago in 1753*

Who knows the engraver and naturalist Thomas Bewick? He has long been admired by those interested in the history of wood engraving and natural history. But many more will have become aware of him since the televising of Simon Schama's *History of Britain*. He lived in stirring times, and though he was no pamphleteer or orator and moved little from his craftsman's workshop in Newcastle-upon-Tyne, he had Tom Paine's *Rights of Man* on his well-filled bookshelves and he was an acute observer of the radical movements of the day. His response to these and to social injustice, as recorded in his autobiographical *Memoir*, has become of particular interest to some historians of the present day. Schama's text makes much of this, and of Bewick's portrayal of the rural poor in the engraved vignettes that punctuated the texts of his celebrated books of natural history.

Bewick was born 256 years ago in August 1753, at Cherryburn on the south bank of the Tyne, some 12 miles upstream from Newcastle. His father and grandfather had both been tenant farmers and had worked in the same nearby colliery. His *Memoir*, published posthumously by his daughter 34 years after his death in 1828, is now regarded as a minor classic. It gives a delightful account of his childhood and early youth, the memory of which stayed with him throughout his life and informed much of his work. Having early shown a gift for

'O now that the genius of Bewick were mine,' wrote Wordsworth. Ruskin borrowed Bewick drawings for his Oxford Lectures

observation and drawing, he was apprenticed at 14 to the engraver Ralph Beilby in Newcastle. His seven-year term of hard graft at the engraving bench, which involved every kind of work on wood, silver, copper, brass and steel and the making of his tools and preparation of his materials, established the foundation for the unfettered expression of his genius.

He had to 'work for the kitchen' all his days; the wood engraving for which he became renowned and which was to transform 19th-century book illustration was in fact a small part of his daily activity.

The publication of his *General History of Quadrupeds* in 1790 and his two-volume *History of British Birds* in 1797 and 1804, largely produced in his spare time, brought him a national reputation

and increasing business for his workshop. The improvement over earlier works of natural history was so striking that praise was universal. He was referred to in *Blackwood's* magazine as 'the Matchless, Inimitable Bewick'; 'O now that the genius of Bewick were mine,' wrote Wordsworth in 1800; Ruskin borrowed Bewick drawings for his Oxford Lectures.

In Bewick's vignettes – 'tale-pieces', he sometimes called them – the narrative content, the ironic, wry observation, the gritty, unsentimental record of the rural scene and its sturdy inhabitants, often battered by rough weather, have always inspired the greatest affection and admiration. Bewick's intention was to

create diversions 'of gaiety and humour, yet even in these seldom without an endeavour to illustrate some truth, or point some moral...' Irony is often present: blind men are led past warning signs by illiterate boys, a donkey scratches its backside against a tottering monument to a futile war, a man pees against a fragment of Hadrian's Wall. And there are warnings: a gibbet in the background to a scene of cruelty by small boys; the legend above the crumbling fireplace of a roofless cottage: 'Did youth but know what age would crave.'

The scenes of desperate rural poverty and social inequality are not so numerous as might be deduced from Schama's nonetheless perceptive text. The figure described as a blind old crofter slurping gruel in a wretched garret is in fact used by Bewick as a shaft at false piety: saying an overlong grace with his eyes shut allows the man's cat to get first to the bowl; the smart young sportsman

is not pointing an imperious dismissal, but enquiring – not of a vagrant but of a resting shepherd – where good shooting might be found. But some of his images are deliberately enigmatic and we must make what we can of them.

Much more could be said of the great variety of work that went through Bewick's workshop, of his 20-year partnership with his former master, of his many apprentices, several of whom went on to success in London, of his talented brother John, and of his son and three

daughters, all of whom died unmarried. A great deal has survived of Bewick's workshop records, his drawings and his correspondence, which despite an extensive literature has been little used until recently. Celebrated in his lifetime, his reputation has never dwindled, and his name remains prominent in every history of his craft.

● *More information on the Bewick Society website, www.bewicksociety.org.*

The Hare (left) and the Harrier (below left) are taken from Bewick's *General History of Quadrupeds*. The Fieldfare (below) and all the other images are from his *History of British Birds*. Opposite: portrait of Bewick by James Ramsey (1816), reproduced courtesy of the Natural History Society of Northumbria.

A driven man

PHOTOGRAPH BY JEFF C

It is a sobering experience to have a book you wrote nearly 40 years earlier suddenly reissued as a 'classic'. This happened to me with the republication in paperback of *Bluebird and the Dead Lake*, my eye-witness account of Donald Campbell's 1964 attempt on the world land speed record. Bluebird was Donald's bright blue 5,000-horsepower car, and the Dead Lake was Lake Eyre, a 30-mile-long stretch of white salt in the great Australian nowhere, 400 miles north of Adelaide, in which, against all conceivable dangers and disasters, he finally achieved the world land speed record of 403 mph.

Rereading those neat sentences written by somebody I barely recognise today, I feel myself being cata-

In the Australian desert, Donald Campbell finally succeeded in beating his father's world land speed record. But even that did not satisfy him, recalls **JOHN PEARSON**

pulted back to that strange Australian summer. I had been sent there by the *Sunday Times*, but in those days I was a snooty young would-be-intellectual, and Donald Campbell was one of the last men on earth with whom I'd have chosen to pass a long hot summer in the Ozzie outback.

The first few days, spent sleeping and eating a dead sheep in a corrugated-iron shack on the Muloorina sheep station, did little to change my mind. The whole enterprise struck me as utterly absurd, and so did Donald. The Australian press had turned against him, the British press tended to ignore him, and behind his back some of the back-up staff already called him 'Biggles'. I nearly did myself – but then I began to alter my opinions.

The first thing that dawned on me was this lunatic's extraordinary courage. I remember sitting in Bluebird's cockpit, and getting the shivers as I gazed through the tiny windscreen at the 18 miles of arctic whiteness down which he'd have to drive this terrifying vehicle at something near half the speed of sound.

I began to see that Donald had something more than courage. It was the quality the Italians call *grinta*, which combines guts, leadership and sheer bloody-minded perseverance. Shackleton had it; so, in a different way, did his arch-rival Scott. Donald shared their ability to shake off disillusion and despair and all those things that catch you in the middle of the night. Not for nothing did Napoleon say that 'the true courage is the courage of 2 am'.

Almost every day Donald had to beat off some fresh setback, as criticisms mounted, money dwindled and parts of the salt lake started to disintegrate from unexpected rains, turning what should have been an ideal surface into a death-trap. He'd managed to convince his big financial backers, he'd built the car, and mounted this whole expensive operation in one of the least hospitable spots on earth: now he had no alternative except to deliver.

'Old boy,' he said to me one night, when it seemed as if the crystallising salt might rip his tyres apart at the speeds at which he had to go, 'it looks as if it's shit or bust.'

The trouble wasn't just the surface of the salt. It was Donald as well. Four years before, while driving Bluebird in a previous record bid on the Bonneville salt flats at Utah, the car had left the track and nearly crashed, leaving him seriously concussed. For several months he lost his nerve, and he still had problems.

As Richard Williams writes in his splendid introduction to my book, what I was watching wasn't 'simply an attempt to drive a motor car faster than one had ever done before', it was also 'the trial of a man'. It was a trial that he won triumphantly.

But the real trial of Donald Campbell still wasn't over. From earliest childhood, he had been living in the shadow of his dominating father, Sir Malcolm Campbell, the most famous record-breaker of his day. In a succession of high-powered cars and motorboats, all called Blue-

Donald grew up worshipping and fearing his father, and did his best to follow his example – but it never really worked

bird, Sir Malcolm had made himself the fastest man alive on land and water. Donald grew up worshipping and fearing him, and did his best to follow his example, not only as a record-breaker, but also with his womanising, his high living and his insouciant attitude to life.

But it never really worked. Donald was a kinder, more sensitive character than his debonair old dad, and the glamorous, pioneering days of speed were nearly over.

In spite of this, I'm convinced that at Lake Eyre Donald was using his Blue-

bird to lay his father's ghost, beating at his own game the handsome martinet who had given him such hell in his childhood. When, against enormous odds, he won his precious record, I believe he was satisfied at last.

But the story hadn't ended. It had been scripted over 2,000 years before by Sophocles, and since Oedipus was punished by the gods for presumption and the sin of parricide, Donald still had to meet his fate. Some months later, back in England, I remember spending a day with him at his house near Reigate and being shown the jet-propelled boat, inevitably named Bluebird too, in which he was planning an attempt on the water speed record. It looked a very doubtful object in which to belt across a lake at something approaching 300 mph. I sensed that Donald felt the same.

'Of course, I realise it might well kill me,' he said.

'Why on earth do it then?' I asked.

'Got to, old chum. Got to. Father held the land and water speed records simultaneously. I intend to do the same.'

I saw little of him after that as I went to live abroad. Early in 1967 I was walking down the Via del Corso in Rome when I spotted the afternoon edition of *Il Messaggero* with the headline, '*Campbell e morto*'. I remember sitting in a cafe and reading about how his wretched boat had somersaulted earlier that day on Coniston Water, leaving no trace behind of Donald, and thinking to myself that in the end it was the father who had killed the son, not vice versa.

'Sir, our cleaner has won the lotter... Oh, you already know'

Olden Life

Who was... The Great Omi?

I BUMPED INTO the world's most tattooed man on a dark winter's night, and he looked so terrifying that I thought he was the devil.

Our encounter took place in 1948 in the deserted stable yard of my father's hotel in a small Border town. I'd been out riding and, carrying a paraffin lamp because there was no electricity in the stables, was heading across the cobbles towards the kitchen door when a figure stepped out of a caravan parked in a corner. I froze with horror when I saw that his shaven head and face were covered with broad zebra-style whorls of black and white. He smiled, and showed teeth filed to points like a piranha fish's. Huge plugs of ivory were stuck through the septum of his nose and his earlobes, and the hand he held out towards me in reassurance had long, curving fingernails like the talons of a giant cat.

It took brandy to restore me to anything like calm – after which I discovered that the terrifying apparition was the Great Omi, one of the attractions at the ancient hiring fair which was still held every February in our town. My father, who loved eccentrics, had plied him with food and drink and invited him to park his van in the yard behind our house.

Sitting at our kitchen table, telling us his story, the Great Omi turned out to be a courteous gentleman with an accent we thought of as 'posh'. He also struck me as a tragic figure, and that is how he has remained in my memory.

His name was Horace Ridler and he had been born in 1892. He served as a major in the First World War; after 1918 he joined the Indian Army, but was either cashiered or resigned – he was vague about the reason. When young he had been 'a bit of a bounder'. During his time in the East he had had some

The Great Omi: 'a courteous gentleman with an accent we thought of as "posh"'

A tattooist was prepared to undertake the work, but only if Ridler had the agreement of his fiancée

small tattoos done by tribesmen either in Burma or Borneo. Casting around for a new way to make a living in the 1920s, he came up with the idea of turning himself into the world's most tattooed man.

A London-based tattooist, 'Professor' George Burchett, was prepared to undertake the work, but only if Ridler had the agreement of his fiancée. Gladys also came from a refined background and, though initially appalled at the idea, she

went ahead with the marriage and travelled with him, calling herself Omette and taking the tent money from curious people eager to see a freak.

Burchett's tattooing work had to be executed in wide sweeps and broad bands to conceal the previous designs on Ridler's body and was extremely painful. It took nearly ten years, 500 sessions and several thousand pounds to complete, but when it was finished every part of his body was covered with huge black whorls – even, it was rumoured, his penis.

He rarely went out in public, but when he did, he covered his head and face with a monkish cowl, partly not to give the curious a free show and partly not to frighten the children.

He showed himself off for money all over the world, enjoying great popularity in America where he appeared on Broadway. He also became one of the favourite sideshows in Bertram Mills's and Barnum and Bailey's circuses

We never heard from him again, to my father's great regret, but when my children were small I used to regale them with the story of the meeting with the devil in the stable yard.

But this year, my daughter sent me a postcard she found in New York of the Great Omi. It showed him exactly as I remembered him, dignified and proud, but it was not his tattoos that struck me most forcibly – it was his strangely vulnerable, sad eyes. I discovered through the internet that Horace Ridler retired from the great show world in the Fifties and he died in a village in Sussex in 1969.

Does anyone else remember him?

LIZ TAYLOR

'**S**orry, Alice, it'd only be a balls-up,' was Joan Littlewood's ambiguous reaction when I wrote to her requesting an interview. Did she think I would balls it up, or that she would? After weeks of pestering, a meeting was arranged at the flat of her long-time friend Peter Rankin in North London, where she stays whenever she comes over from her home in Paris.

Now 87, Joan Littlewood hates interviews and hasn't done one for years. 'I don't see much point,' she complains, 'I never did talk much about what I was doing.' She is standing apprehensively in the living room and, despite looking a little more frail than she did in the Stratford East days, it is unmistakably Joan, dressed simply in shirt, cardigan and trademark trousers and sailor's cap. Feisty and sharp as ever, she is appalled when I ask if Jane Bown, the *Oldie* photographer, has been. 'What, I don't want my bloody photograph taken! I'm not a bloody actress!'

Despite her humble background – she was brought up by her working-class grandparents in Stockwell – Joan's voice is quite posh, yet still carries traces of old cockney patter. Her sentences are peppered with expletives, which entertain rather than shock, and when she smiles (revealing that distinctive gap between her teeth), her shrewd eyes, like a wily old mandarin's, light up with amusement.

Apart from being bitter about various institutions that have obstructed her work (the Arts Council, the GLC, the BBC), she can be hilariously rude about theatre's sacred cows and won't mince her words when attacking anyone she sees as devoid of talent, from Andrew Lloyd Webber ('That *Cats* put the kiss of death on music') and Wolf Mankowitz ('He never did anything original') to Laurence Olivier ('Another one that couldn't act').

When it comes to discussing herself, Joan is at first reticent and self-effacing. I ask her which achievement she is most proud of, and she replies that she has never achieved anything, but simply loved working the way she did. Considering she is one of our most original and influential theatrical directors, this comes as a surprise. Extraordinary to think that her world-famous Theatre Workshop (a reformed version of the left-wing touring company she set up with her husband Ewan MacColl in the 1930s) started life in the derelict Theatre Royal in East London half a century ago.

Carving a niche very much outside the theatrical establishment, it was here

Joan Littlewood

The theatre director and founder of the ground-breaking Theatre Workshop gives **ALICE PITMAN** *a rare and typically forthright interview. Photograph by* **JANE BOWN**

at Stratford that Joan worked to her own unique, often improvisational, methods encouraging audience participation and concentrating on productions of little-known plays.

Alongside her lifelong companion and endlessly resourceful manager Gerry Raffles, Joan nurtured an impressive and innovative stable of mainly working-class actors and actresses, most of whom went on to figure large in almost every notable English TV sitcom and drama in subsequent years. This has not always made Joan happy. Very much a creature of the theatre, Joan has no time for television, seeing it as a medium that has stifled rather than liberated the full potential of her beloved actors.

'A wonderful actor like Harry Corbett in that shitty old *Steptoe* every week, and that silly old man with him! It was

terrible,' she complains.

Isn't she curious to know how her protégé Barbara Windsor is getting on in *EastEnders*? (*Sparrows Can't Sing*, starring Barbara Windsor, was the only film Joan ever directed.) 'Oh, I know how she's getting on, the little bitch. I love her. She's very bright, she's a bloody good actress.'

Harry H Corbett, Yootha Joyce, Brian Murphy, Lionel Bart, Roy Kinnear, James Booth, Victor Spinetti ... the exciting young talent produced by the Theatre Workshop was endless. But Joan didn't recruit just anyone. She turned down Sean Connery because she didn't think he was any good. 'Nearly eight years he tried to join us and I wouldn't have him. He was terrible! There's another one who wanted to join us... I forget these buggers' names... It was so long ago... An East End fellow who's taken another name. Peter will know...' Joan calls for

Peter who pokes his head round the door. 'Peter, what was the name of that fuck-face from the East End – the one I told to go to Hollywood?'

'Michael Caine,' says Peter.

'Michael Caine! That's the one. Years later, he would go around saying it was the best bit of bloody advice he ever had!' Joan chuckles, her eyes agleam with mischief. Does she ever regret turning these two cinema giants down? 'Absolutely not: they couldn't act for toffee.'

Apart from her instinctive talent for spotting potential in her actors, Joan Littlewood also knew a good play when she saw one, and would frequently take on new writing that no one else would touch. In 1958 she directed Brendan Behan's *The Hostage*, which eventually transferred to the West End. 'Brendan was incomparable,' says Joan. 'My Gerry kept him alive another two years, but you see, the Irish tend to laugh at somebody when they're drunk. I loved him. He used to call me the English Sinn Fein – he'd attack the English, I'd attack the Irish, or I'd attack the English, and he'd attack the Irish!'

Later came the phenomenal success of Shelagh Delaney's *A Taste of Honey*. A 19-year-old from the back streets of Salford, Shelagh Delaney decided to write her own play after seeing a Terence Rattigan production at the Opera House, where she worked as an usherette.

'She went home saying' (Joan adopts a deadpan Salford accent) '"I reckon I could write as well as that." She wrote while her father lay ill in bed. It didn't have any shape, and no real ending, yet there was this thing that I loved, this touch of truth that you didn't really hear in the theatre – ordinary working-class stuff, nothing pretentious.'

Brendan Behan once remarked that both he and Shelagh Delaney were products of Joan Littlewood's imagination. What did Joan think he meant by that?

'I did an awful lot to improve their work. I have imagination. I know I how theatre works. I can write and I can adapt. I did a lot of work on that beautiful *Quare Fellow* of his. For example, he'd have the hangman tell nine jokes, and I'd say "Brendan, I'm sorry, you can't have nine jokes! You can have one!"'

Joan suddenly looks very sad. 'Brendan was special, he really was. Success killed him, because before he hadn't the money to get drunk. I was so angry with Brendan for dying, I felt like kicking the coffin.'

When she invited the ordinary people of Stratford to watch rehearsals of *Oh, What a Lovely War!* – her savage satire based on the First World War – she first had an inkling of the great impact the musical was going to have. 'They'd come in and watch and wouldn't want to go, and we even put some of their stories into the production. It really was theatre of the people,' she adds with passion. 'It touched a nerve in England. It was done with great simplicity and belief, and I knew it was something special.'

Joan displays a healthy reluctance to analyse the immense success of the Theatre Workshop. Despite explaining her policy of not having any casting and of banning critics or loved ones from rehearsals, she seems as baffled as anyone else. Perhaps it boils down to her earlier admission that she simply understood how to make theatre work.

> **'What was the name of that fuckface from the East End – the one I told to go to Hollywood? Michael Caine, that's the one!'**

Would Joan agree that, despite her own efforts, most working-class people in this country still don't go to the theatre? 'Of course they don't! Yet there could be gorgeous theatre in every corner. But it takes backing. We never went near the posh places, they wouldn't have had me anyway, but we'd play in miners' halls and I'd get the job of minding the babies so the women could go.'

'It's a shame', I say, 'that there doesn't seem to be anyone around today with the same drive to bring theatre to the people.'

'How do you know there isn't!' Joan fires back. There could be someone doing that right now, as we speak!'

Does she still consider herself a left-wing idealist? 'I'm not a left-wing idealist!' she exclaims indignantly. 'I've always been a communist. I know things go wrong, of course they do. But we didn't go wrong. We didn't sell out.'

Just before I go, my seven-year-old son is mentioned and Joan, aghast at not having known about him before, rifles through books and papers trying to find something for him. I wondered if she ever regrets not having children of her own. She turns round and in a proud voice devoid of any mawkish sentiment replies: 'My actors were my children.'

'Sure, I got my people to talk to your people – turned out they were the same people'

Painting and decorating
in Shekhawati

Ilay Cooper immersed himself in the unique and colourful murals of Rajasthan, India, and in them found a novel approach to story-telling...

Thirty-five years ago, I pushed a bike through the tiny paved streets of Taranagar in rural Rajasthan and, without realising it, entered the beginning of the rest of my life. All around was desert, and above me loomed great mansions (known as havelis) covered with paintings – the show of wealth seemed utterly incongruous to me at that time.

In northern Rajasthan, a merchant class had flourished on cross-desert trade, until, that is, the British transformed the trade patterns. These merchants then moved 1,000 miles east to Calcutta, to corner the market in textiles and opium. By the late 19th century, however, vast fortunes were flowing home. They built big in a competitive riot of conspicuous wealth. Havelis, temples, cenotaphs, wells and caravanserais rose and, as a final touch, each was covered with pictures. (After Independence, those adaptable emigrant merchants invest-

The pictures are clever, amusing, crazy and mysterious

ed in the manufacturing industries left vacant by the departing British. Known as Marwaris, they now hold some 50 per cent of India's industrial capital.)

The pictures themselves are clever, amusing, crazy and mysterious. I was fascinated, and, from my base in Churu, cycled out to define borders, ask questions and simply to look. I am now the authority on the genre.

The merchants, or Marwaris, bought art by the square metre; the painters, masons with talent, picked the décor. At first, they used earthy reds and greens in a vernacular fresco technique, their pictures flat, spare and lively.

New German pigments, ultramarine and chrome red, shifted the palette, while prints introduced Victorian realism, transforming the vision. The pictures grew cluttered and, with their new colours, became gaudy, losing aesthetically but retaining vivacity.

Opposite page, main picture: Princess Alexandra averts her eyes from the sexy scene beside her, Churi Ajitgarh. *Inset*: Rear of an 1890s Kanhaiyalal Bagla Haveli, Churu. *This page, clockwise from left*: A man adjusts his sound system, Churu; Trains on a haveli built c.1930; Cycling to the call box, Mandawa; Ships were alien to the desert painter – for English he relied on his paint tin, this time held upside-down, Sardarshahr.

Folk stories are generally a popular theme. When love stories cross caste or religious barriers, they end sadly; otherwise it is a struggle to happily-ever-after. A scene from Dhola-Maru, a Rajasthani tale commonly portrayed, shows Dhola controlling their camel as Maru holds off bandits with a stream of arrows. Small beer for her: she had already died and been resurrected.

Foreigners first intrude on the walls as mercenaries, then armies; a procession of soldiers in alien uniforms. Their odd contraptions follow: paddle steamers carrying the merchants' goods up the Ganges, and then the trains that replaced them, provide a marvellous horizontal frieze. Balloons fly, it seems, only thanks to passengers blowing into a tube. An early plane is labelled a 'flying ship', and there are cars and bicycles galore. Each, it seems, is better imagined rather than copied.

The painters copied, with or without adapting. A print of the Sacred Heart omitted the cigar from Jesus's heavenward pointing fingers: our painter put that right. Picture labels promoting British textile companies, carefully reproduced, include the company name and blanks for bale length and batch number. When copying 'Made in Germany' along the hull of a ship, the artist, sadly, held his paint tin the wrong way up…

Erotica is fun, but slyly placed. In each new town I'd find a naughty-looking teenage guide. He'd know. A couple, half-clad, hard at work in a railway carriage; a woman displaying her all behind a bracket; horses mating; a young fellow looking shyly over his shoulder as he holds his – ah, only his finger; a man ravishing a donkey (the label makes it a mare. This last detail is important: I never found any gay gallivanting.)

They chose sex and royals for a room in Churi Ajitgarh – Victoria, deep in mourning, and Princess Alexandra alternate with nights of bliss: not satire, just pretty. The comeuppance? There are two murals of women giving birth in Mandawa.

When tourism developed, Mandawa became its focus. The French and Spanish love Shekhawati. The British usually pass by; like Abraham Lockett, whose 1831 report set the ball rolling and lead to the suppression of local banditry. Conspicuous wealth then became safer. Two final Robin Hoods succumbed outside Mahansar in 1926, their memorial falsely blaming British bullets – it was unseemly for martial Rajputs to kill one another. They feature in the last of the pictures, which were painted before the merchants, now industrialists, forsook Shekhawati.

GETTING AROUND

A hired car is best for exploring. Mandawa, central to Shekhawati, is 275km from Delhi, and 170km from Jaipur. Direct buses, and less direct trains, serve almost all towns.

Good accommodation and painted buildings can be found in Mandawa, Jhunjhunu, Mahansar, Nawalgarh and Fatehpur. I prefer Mahansar's fort, Narayan Niwas Castle or Hotel Shiv Shekhawati in Jhunjhunu.

The best guide is mine: *The Painted Towns of Shekhawati*, 3rd edition, due soon from Prakash Publishing, New Delhi.

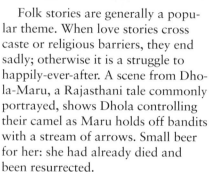

I was a teenage columnist!

I was young and inexperienced with nothing to say, yet I spoke to the nation...

Decca Aitkenhead

When I was 22 and still an undergraduate, I got a part-time job at the *Manchester Evening News*. I had only been there a few weeks when the features editor spotted me by the coffee machine and asked if I'd mind standing in for a columnist.

The same thing happened a year later when I started at the *Independent*. Then it happened again, at the *Independent on Sunday*, and by the time I was 25 I found I had a weekly column on the comment pages of the *Guardian*. I remember thinking it surprising that not one editor had asked me what I wanted to say with a column, nor how I could be considered qualified for the job.

To my regret, I don't remember asking myself either. A column is so unquestioningly prized as the lottery win of journalism that you would have to be out of your mind, it is said, to turn one down.

Not one editor asked me what I wanted to say with a column. To my regret, I didn't ask myself either

It took the best part of ten years to realise that this is just one of the many mistaken ideas people have about being a columnist.

The first common misapprehension is that the words which appear on the page were written in conditions of absolute creative freedom. 'Your own column,' people marvel. 'So you can write whatever you like?' The only constraint that ever occurs to anyone is an imagined pressure to express opinions with which the editor agrees. 'You probably have to toe the party line, eh?' people will sometimes suggest, knowingly. Funnily enough, this is the only problem I have never encountered. The real constraints on a columnist are a great deal more restrictive than that, and infinitely more soul-destroying.

When you write a column, the first thing you need is a 'peg'; a news event which makes your opinion topical. You can't write about, say, capital punishment just because you think it's interesting. It has to be in the news. As a rule of thumb, your peg should be no more than three days old, and ideally less than 24 hours. Entirely at the mercy of events, you are employed as a definitive voice of authority on matters about which until yesterday you might never have given a thought.

A peg cannot be just any news item, however. It must be sufficiently high profile to merit a column's attention. But the bigger the story, the busier the turf; columnists are all fighting over the same raw material, and if someone else gets an opinion into print first, then no matter how passionate or ingenious your version might have been, it is not going to be published.

Then there is the question of whether you yourself have previously argued the same point. The number of newsworthy opinions in existence is surprisingly finite, and if you do the job for long enough you will inevitably find that old ones begin to recycle. Repetition troubles some columnists less than others. Some years ago, when the *Guardian* accidentally reprinted the same column by Hugo Young on consecutive weeks, Young himself had to point out the error, because no one else had even noticed. The good humour in which he took the mishap was rightly admired as a mark of his 'professionalism' – but it is a professionalism to which one wouldn't necessarily want to aspire.

By the time you have worked through this process of elimination, the subject at which you arrive for your column is often one on which you would never have imagined yourself writing. But there's nothing else for it; the space has to be filled. In these circumstances, overcompensation is almost inevitable, and the next day you open the paper to find you've impersonated someone who cares passionately about *Celebrity Big Brother* or Camilla Parker Bowles.

'Got anything in the diplomatic corps, baldy?'

'Have you any idea how many sea turtles have been trapped in shrimp nets while we've been enjoying ourselves?'

There are rare weeks, of course, when fortune smiles. A big story has broken about which you know something, and you have a fresh, important comment to offer. But even then there is no guarantee of a happy ending, because you still face another challenge – negotiating the constant, delicate tension between being a credible and consistent commentator, and becoming a bore. On the whole, your views should broadly chime with those of your readers. They should also reflect a coherent world view. On the other hand, it is no good preaching to the converted all the time; it is essential, therefore, to occasionally write something wholly unexpected, highly controversial, and probably completely indefensible. Like jokers, these columns are wild cards for you to deploy to shake things up.

And here we come to the fundamental faultline of the job. Put simply, your boss wants more jokers than you do. A comment editor loves nothing more than to stir up a mighty rumpus.

When the cleverest editors are discussing what to write about with a columnist, they coax recklessness by implying one of two things: a) that a plainly lunatic argument is actually pretty innocuous; or b) that once readers have got over their shock and outrage, the devastating logic of your bold counter-blast will be so irresistible that they'll be forced to agree. Either way the editor makes the columnist feel that together you are a team – a daring partnership, ready to brave public controversy side by side.

So you write something crazy. You feel slightly giddy afterwards, but the editor is thrilled, and at least the thing is over and done with for the week. It is only when you wake up the next day to 500 abusive readers' emails and your phone won't stop ringing with invitations from radio stations to 'defend your controversial

views on air', that you remember that your editor's name – your trusty partner in crime – doesn't actually appear on the by-line. The only name is yours. If his name comes into it at all, it will only be when he publishes a mealymouthed apology on the letters page the following day, distancing himself and the newspaper from the irresponsible ravings of a rogue columnist.

Despite all of this, some journalists have mastered the art being a columnist. They have enough knowledge in the bank to be able to produce informed comment at short notice. They have enough confidence to withstand the pressure of excitable editors, and enough judgement to play their jokers shrewdly. These columnists can be many things, but what they all are, crucially, and quite obviously, is old.

This seems glaringly apparent. Bizarrely, however, editors today have a perverse infatuation with young columnists, founded on the unsound notions that young columnists will attract young readers, and that old readers are fascinated by what young people think. So they scan their newsroom, spot the youngest face in the office, and feel their pulse quicken. 'There it is – the voice of youth! Give that youth a column!' And thus another column goes to the very journalist least qualified for the job.

Question Time, Newsnight, Radio 4, they can't leave young columnists alone – not because what they write is any good, but because they are just so deliciously, thrillingly young. It's hardly surprising that before they reach thirty so many are already finished, discredited by all the silly things they've said about subjects they knew nothing about. Their novelty fades, everyone notices what nonsense they spout – and anyway, by then, of course, they're too old.

RANT

RAYMOND BRIGGS *has had enough of annoying signs...*

HAMPSHIRE – FOR QUALITY OF LIFE says the road sign on the border. Quality? What quality? Good quality? Poor quality? 'Never mind the quality, feel the width' of Hampshire. Are there no unemployed in Hampshire, no drugs, no crime?

HAYWARDS HEATH ♥ OF MID-SUSSEX. If that place is the heart, heaven help the rest of Sussex.

Who writes this garbage? More importantly, why? A battered old builder's lorry proclaims on its side: **SUPPLYING THE CUTTING EDGE.** The cutting edge of what? Bricks? Sand and cement?

'The **SERVICE** standing at Platform 4...' A 'service' can't stand anywhere. It's a train, for God's sake. And we are not 'customers', we are passengers. Also, the next **STATION STOP** is a station. That's what stations are for, isn't it? It's where the trains stop. Don't they know that?

THANK YOU FOR TRAVELLING WITH SOUTHERN. What the hell else are we going to do? Walk the fifty miles from Brighton? Hire a helicopter? Hop on a bus for two or three hours?

And those vans in London – **RUNNING WATER FOR YOU.** So clever! The copywriter must have dined out on that one. Down here they are not running water for us, they are running it for Australians. Our South East Water was bought by the Frogs who then flogged it to the Australians.

RUNNING WATER FOR AUSSIE SHAREHOLDERS. They don't put that on the vans. No wonder we've had a drought. They've got deserts out there, haven't they?

George Bush Snr

I was in Bangkok with a team of volunteer doctors and nurses on a mission to restore sight to Thai patients and teach Thai doctors sight-saving skills, when I received a fax from my chairman, Mr Leonard McCollum, founder of Conoco Oil, telling me to return immediately to the United States as we had an appointment with Vice-President Bush in Washington the following day. I was the executive director of Orbis, an international charity, and part of my responsibility was to raise $10 million a year, the annual operating budget. I had asked Mr McCollum if he could arrange a meeting with George Bush so I could ask him to continue the $3 million a year support from the US government. Mr McCollum was an old oil business friend of his.

Twenty-four hours later, in a Washington hotel, I met Mr McCollum, an 85-year-old Texan, and his wife Eleanor, a charming but somewhat overbearing and enthusiastic born-again Christian. Also in the group was my other chairman, Al Ueltschi, a much younger and very successful businessman, another Texan and my working boss. Neither Eleanor McCollum nor Mr Ueltschi had ever met George Bush, so this was a big moment for them and me. As we waited for the limousine I had organised to take us to Bush's office, the discussion went like this. 'Well, Oliver, what are we gonna tell the Vice-President? I don't rightly know what we're gonna say.'

'Oh, praise Jesus, we are going to meet George Bush, the Viiiice President. Praise Jesus! Oh Oliver, isn't it great? Jesus is alive!' exclaimed Eleanor joyfully.

'Well, Oliver, you know what to say – don't you?' said Mr Ueltschi.

'I'll be happy to inform him of our work over the past five years and the blind we have helped,' I said.

'Oh, praise Jesus. You, Oliver, have helped bliiind people, just like Jesus.

Above: George Bush Snr at the White House with (left to right) Al Ueltschi, Oliver Foot and Eleanor and Leonard McCollum

McCollum turned to his wife to introduce her to the Vice President. 'I'd like you to meet... er, er, ah, er...'

You're so wonderful,' said Eleanor. I was heavily jet-lagged, and this surreal scene was hard to grasp.

The limousine should have arrived: it was 2 pm and our meeting was at 2.30. I went off to check, but it was nowhere to be seen. The limo company told me not to worry. 'The limo's on its way – I just called them,' I announced as I rejoined my nervous group in the lounge of the hotel. 'Damn well better be, or you're in trouble,' said Mr Ueltschi, who never had a problem speaking his mind.

'Uh-uh-uh, what's going on?' said Mr McCollum, a little confused. 'The car's on its way,' I said. 'Oh yeah – we're going to see George, aren't we?'

Another five minutes went by. 'Look, Oliver, this is the one time when your organisational skills have to work. Where's the damn limo?' Mr Ueltschi barked. I called again, and was told that the limo had broken down and wasn't going to make it. I ran back to my group. 'The limo has broken down. We'll have to get a regular cab. We should go now.' 'Hell, Oliver, what's the matter with you – don't you realise this meeting could mean money?' Ueltschi screamed as we made our way to the lobby. 'Oh, it's the DEVIL, I know it's

the Devil – he doesn't want us to meet the Vice-President,' cried Mrs McCollum. 'What's going on?' said Mr McCollum as he shuffled along behind us.

I hailed a yellow cab. 'Take us to the Old Executive Office as fast as possible.' 'Where's that?' the driver asked. 'IT'S THE DEVIL – WE ARE GOING TO BE LATE – OH LORD FORGIVE US!' shrieked Mrs McCollum.

We arrived at Bush's office at 2.45. We sat in silence in the anteroom. A grandfather clock ticked loudly. A beautiful Texan secretary picked up the phone and in a Texan drawl said, 'Uh-huh. Uh-huh. Uh-huh. Uuuuu-huh!' She put the phone down and announced: 'Vice-President Bush will not be able to see you...' – 'IT'S THE DEVIL, THE DEVIL!!! I KNEW HE WOULD WIN!!' cried Eleanor – '...he will not be able to see you in this office but will meet with you in the White House.'

'PRAISE JESUS! HE HAS OVERCOME!' screamed Eleanor.

We were escorted underground and into another lift that took us up into the White House. Famous people were milling around and being received by President Reagan and George Bush in their separate offices, where they were honoured for their good works. People came out of Reagan's office, and as they

'What would go well with beans on toast?'

walked by Eleanor jumped up from her seat. 'I would like you to meet Oliver Foot. He's just like Jesus. He goes around the world and SAVES BLIIIND PEOPLE.'

Al Ueltschi and McCollum were having an argument about the best way to raise cattle. 'The best way to breed a good bull is to use artificial insemination – you can choose the best sperm,' Ueltschi argued. 'No, no, no! The only way and the best way is to give 'em the real thing! I mean the real thing. Get a good bull to do it! Nothing can beat the real jab!!' McCollum fought back.

'The Vice-President will see you now,' another blonde Texan announced, and she strutted ahead, leading the way. The door to Bush's office was open. He was standing behind his desk. 'Good to see you, Mac,' said Bush, walking up and shaking McCollum's hand. 'I'm happy to meet with you any time, Mac. We have been through a whole bunch together. They were the good old days.'

McCollum turned to his wife to introduce her. 'I'd like you to meet my wife, er, er, ah, er…' He looked at Eleanor. Then, quick as a flash, it came to him – 'my dear wife, Eleanor.' Eleanor went up to Bush, grabbed him by the shoulders and kissed him on both cheeks. 'This is a great moment for me. It's my honour.' Red lipstick was smudged on both the Vice-President's cheeks.

Then it was Al Ueltschi's turn. There was a long pause. Al Ueltschi is a difficult one, I thought. 'George, I would like you to meet my good friend… er, er…' – a pause, and then it came, albeit somewhat slurred – 'Al Ulshi.' Al Ueltschi stepped up and shook his hand. It was the moment of his life.

Finally it was my turn. Mr McCollum looked at me and his face was a complete blank. 'And this… er, er, er, young man, er, er – he runs the thing. Er…' Pause. 'Er, ah, er…' Pause. Should I jump in and introduce myself? Al Ueltschi shuffled, as if to give a hint of my name.

'Er, er…' McCollum's eyes were completely vacant.But slowly his face began to change, and he got it. Looking directly at me, he turned to Bush and said, 'I would like you to meet OLIVER [pause] TWIST, the son of Lord and Lady Godiva,' he said victoriously.

As I shook Mr Bush's hand I whispered: 'Foot is the name, and my father is Lord Caradon.' 'I know, I know,' he whispered.

The good news is that we got the $3 million. **OLIVER FOOT**

ANORAK
FLASH WILSON

I AM A SELF-CONFESSED pylonphile. Yes, I run the Pylon Appreciation Society. As a result, I've come to meet some interesting people (and admittedly some who are rather dull). However, mostly it's the desperate mothers of ten-year-old boys who get in touch, so I created the Society for them (complete with badge and poster). Members get access to a special 'spotter's guide' featuring a different model every month.

My passion started when I saw the National Grid privatisation adverts on TV during the Eighties, where electricity pylons strode across the landscape, putting the world to rights. I realised that pylons resemble people – with arms, legs and a head – and that while many resent their presence, we should actually appreciate their giant benign companionship. After all, everyone wants to use electricity and it has to be carried to our houses by something.

As I looked at pylons I began to realise that they weren't all the same – there are different designs to go around corners, over rivers, into substations and across hills – and my spark of interest grew to a current.

I started a website – a photo gallery of 'Pylons around the world' – and found that I'm not the only one with this strange hobby. I receive lots of questions from readers – most commonly, 'Can pylons cause cancer?', to which my answer is that currently there is no known scientific way that it is possible, and that for every piece of research suggesting a link, there's another to disprove it.

'What are your favourite pylons?' is much easier for me to answer. There are a set of three, one a design I've never seen elsewhere, in a village called Cressing in Essex. They route one line under another from a substation, and the pylons are in a field near the main road through the village. It's hard to explain what I like about these in particular; partly their uniqueness and partly because they are pleasing on the eye. But for me, all pylons have a certain drama. Close up, they are quite imposing, and on a humid day you can often hear the wires crackle, potent.

Let me share some pylon trivia with you:
• The tallest pylons in the UK span the Thames at Thurrock. At 610 feet high they are even taller than the Post Office tower.
• In 1928, architect Sir Reginald Blomfield chose the pylon design first used by the CEGB from competition entries.
• Each pylon is uniquely numbered, bearing its own name plate.
• In the post-war era, pylons were seen as a positive symbol. There is a public information film, Power and Prosperity, which portrays the erection of new pylons as a fantastic thing, part of the expansion of the National Grid which was required to bring growth and wealth.

My favourite pylon-related activity is to take a regular fluorescent tube and stand below powerlines at night, preferably where there are many high voltage lines together, such as near a substation. The tube will glow in your hands. This phenomenon was also demonstrated by Richard Box in 'Field', an art installation, in March 2004, and it's well-known to us pylon enthusiasts.

You may think I'm a little mad, but while there are pylons, there will be their fans!

'Sorry I'm late. What with Thursday being the new Friday, I thought it was Saturday'

Waiting for Tony

It was a perfect summer afternoon, and **GEORGE PERKIN** *had invited his neighbour to come round for tea in the garden. But Tony never arrived...*

The sun is shining in a faultless blue sky and it is a perfect English summer afternoon. The cushions are laid out on the warm stone bench in my small London garden. The garden itself is enclosed, private, planted with ivy, honeysuckle, box and white roses. Although this is London, there is a curious stillness in the garden, an oasis of calm even though only a few feet away cars jostle for position and block the street. Nothing stirs save for the fluttering of a white butterfly around the white roses. All seems perfect except that something is missing: it lacks a visitor.

So I ring up my friend Tony who lives quite alone in a similar terraced house to mine in the next street. I have known Tony for ten years. I first caught sight of him in his red canoe on the River Thames which winds through our district: a lone figure in silhouette paddling into the sunset. 'Are you doing anything special?' I enquire. 'It seems such a perfect afternoon, I wondered if you'd like a cup of tea in the garden.' 'What a jolly good idea,' he replies, jovial, hearty almost – his habitual rather false cheerful voice. 'Tell you what, though, I'm just finishing some writing. Suppose I ring you in about half an hour – say at quarter to five – and let you know if I'm through?' I say that would be fine. 'Righty-oh, matey,' the mock-jovial voice continues (we were both once in the Navy). 'See you in half an hour.'

I go out into the garden and put two mugs and a plate of biscuits on the table. Then I remember that I've got some cake and I put that out too. I begin to think about Tony. Most people find him impossible – reclusive, critical, argumentative, obsessive, given to pontificating. He can be a terrible bore. So any friends he might have had, including at least three ladies, have long since fled in disarray. For

some reason, I seem to be the only one who has stayed to listen.

His only relative is an elderly mother of 93 in a home in Worthing about whom he is rather rude, but he goes down every weekend on his motorbike to see her; he tells me she once played the piano for silent films. Over the years he has blown hot and cold, sometimes roundly abusive to me, storming out of the house, sometimes passing me by in

> **He usually gives two rings when he's coming and then puts the phone down to save paying for the call**

the street. Then, without warning, the mood will change and something vulnerable, almost gentle, will appear. But I have always sensed someone of intelligence and passion fighting to get out from behind the barricades. On his rooftop he keeps a high-powered telescope through which he surveys the night sky. He is extremely knowledgeable about this. In his good moods he will play his mouth-organ like a charm. To tell the truth, I have somehow grown rather fond of the old stick over the years. And then we both share something in common: we both live alone.

Now in his mid-sixties, a retired surveyor, he bicycles about the street in frayed and greasy denim, speaking to no one, hunting down the cheap reduced items in the supermarket before closing. He actually owns three houses, two of which lie empty, and in all I reckon he's worth a few bob. But he refuses to sell anything and lives like a pauper. The funniest thing he tells me is that the girl next door always has the central heating raging in winter; as the party wall is rather thin, he leans against it to 'feel the benefit', as he puts it, resolutely refusing to put on any heating himself.

It is now 4.45 pm and I wait for the telephone to ring. He usually gives two rings when he's coming and then puts the phone down to save paying for the call. But it doesn't ring and the time goes on to 5 pm and then 5.15. I begin to get annoyed. He has done this to me before, suddenly changing his mind, or going out, or putting the answering machine on if he doesn't want to talk to anyone. I curse him roundly. But five minutes later I decide to ring him myself. 'This is Anthony Petherton...' a voice rather pompously announces. So he has put the answering machine on. 'Look here,

Tony,' I say into the machine, 'are you coming or not, for goodness sake? It's getting late.' No one rings back. I try again after 15 minutes. Anthony Petherton replies. By now, incandescent with rage, I go stamping round to his house and bang on the door. No reply.

It is only then that I notice something odd: his bicycle is leaning against the wall, so he hasn't gone out. Faint alarm bells are set off in my mind. I remember that two years ago there was some talk of a heart scare and he was told to lay off the cigarettes. Since then he has continued to smoke steadily. The alarm bells clang loudly. Turning round I see that the traffic has stopped at the level-crossing gates nearby, and in the queue is a police car. Instinctively I run towards it and say to the young driver, 'Excuse me, but I'm a bit worried about a friend in that house. Could you please have a look?'

The policeman, who looks about seventeen, drives round and is all courtesy. He suggests that perhaps the gentleman has fallen asleep in a chair. I say I doubt it. As the house is terraced and the door is locked, there is no way of getting in. The policeman rings the bell next door and a startled woman in a housecoat appears who finally admits him to her garden so that he can climb over the fence and get in from the back. I wait outside the front door with my heart pounding.

Finally the door opens and the policeman appears. 'I'll just look through the house, sir, if you wouldn't mind waiting outside.' I wait for what seems an eternity. When the policeman reappears, his voice is flat, matter-of-fact, official. 'I'm sorry to say, sir, that the gentleman is dead. Are you a close friend?' The street seems to turn on its axis. Automatically I answer the questions. No, there are no relatives except the mother of 93 in the Worthing home. No, I don't know the address. No, I don't know his doctor or his solicitor. I don't seem to know anything. The policeman tells me that I have done the right thing and gives me his contact number.

I walk slowly home, not quite seeing anything, lurching into a woman with a pram. I unlock my front door and go out into the silent garden. The sun is lower now and is just glancing off the white roses. The white butterfly is still fluttering about. Automatically and without feeling I pick up two mugs, a plate of biscuits and the cake, and put them back in the kitchen cupboard.

NOT MANY DEAD
Important stories you may have missed

While Liverpool soaks up the limelight as this year's European City of Culture, Dudley is fighting back through a newly crowned 59-year-old belly-dancing complementary therapist

RAIN ADDS TO FLOOD THREAT: rain water making its way downstream
Shropshire Star

Singer Paula Abdul has broken her nose after falling while trying to avoid stepping on her pet dog
Shropshire Star

A ground-floor classroom window was cracked at Vigo Junior School in Andover
Andover Advertiser

FATHER AND THREE CHILDREN OKAY AFTER VAN GETS STUCK
Ottowa Citizen

Ian McEwan could become only the third novelist to win the Man Booker Prize for a second time
Metro

WOMAN STRANDED WHEN BUS WAS LATE
Front page of the Mid-Wales Journal

'Another case of "do you know who I am?" came when George Reynolds, the Cherwell district councillor, arrived at Oxford Town Hall last week. He was there deputising for council leader Barry Wood, who was tied up with something more important. He introduced himself at the front desk, but a bemused receptionst replied, "Sorry, who are you?"'
Oxford Mail

Vandalism, Skyline Drive: A woman said her neighbour cut down a bamboo shoot in her backyard.
Laguna News and Post, California

New Year's resolutions in the Daily Telegraph – Robert Harris, novelist. 'Can't think of anything but I've got Richard Ingrams here, so I'll ask him... No, we can't think of anything...'

PARENTS' LOW PAY IS MAIN REASON FOR CHILD POVERTY
Daily Mail

FORMULA ONE STAR CAN'T REMEMBER NATIONAL ANTHEM
Lead story, Stratford Upon Avon Herald

Patients like tea and toast when recovering in hospital because it reminds them of home, says a nursing survey
Daily Mirror

Pride of place

JOHN McEWEN *talked to Peter Brook, 'the Pennine Landscape Painter', on the eve of his 2004 retrospective*

The writer and farmer R W Poole describes his friend Peter Brook, 'the Pennine Landscape Painter', as 'a quiet, shy man, who sums you up before he lets his dry Yorkshire wit loose.' The dry wit can often be found in his pictures: 'Procession with a Distracted Dog and a Baffled Sheep', or 'Just Look at the State of the Bloody Pennines – Wonderful' – because he revels in their return to an unpeopled wilderness.

Peter Brook was born in 1927 and has lived with his wife Mollie in the same semi-detached house on the outskirts of Brighouse for 45 years. His love of the surrounding countryside stems from childhood holidays at his grandparents' Pennine farm: 'My subjects now really go back to when I was a kid. I'm still looking at the same things I liked then – only perhaps a little more intelligently.'

The disarming titles printed in child-like capitals across his pictures add a deceptively naïve touch. He is a graduate of Goldsmith's, and when I asked him what picture by another artist he would most like to own he said a Degas monoprint. 'You can see where he's rubbed the ink with his fingers or wiped or scratched it. Very versatile. Quite poetic – not painted or printed to rules. As he's gone along he's developed a feeling for the picture.'

It might describe Brook's own method. His subjects are so solid-looking it takes scrutiny to see how thinly he paints, how much he suggests rather

His subjects are so solid-looking it takes scrutiny to see how thinly he paints, how much he suggests rather than describes

than describes. For many effects he uses a battered old roller or his fingers.

Brook spent the first half of his career supplementing his income as an art teacher, much of it at the local Sowerby Bridge grammar school – 'a very happy time'. I asked him what he advised his pupils. 'Just take what you think's important and put it in, for a start.'

A picture with one of his longest titles is 'David Hockney Arriving in Bradford to Spend Christmas with his Mother and Design the Cover of the Telephone Directory f.o.c.'. It is meant as a compliment – a desolate and snowy Pennine farm with a dawning yellow sky and pink vapour trail representing the artist flying in from sunny LA. 'I thought I'd make it pretty – Hockney likes pink – but that vapour trail, I had a hell of a job drawing it, it was in and out twenty times before I got the right quality,' he told the art critic Mary Sara, adding that in recent pictures by the notoriously eclectic Hockney there has not 'been enough of his own there'. The opposite could be said of Brook, whose later work invariably includes himself and his sheepdog Shep.

Brook came to the art world's attention with a series of well received shows at Agnew's beginning in 1969, but the

world was already coming to his Pennine door in the form of Tom Courtenay, James Mason and other stars, and his reputation spread by word of mouth. The Hollywood mogul Hal Wallis appeared one afternoon in Brighouse with his entourage and bought fourteen pictures on the spot. 'Amazing, isn't it?' Brook says with unfeigned surprise. 'I've never gone out of my way to creep around anybody.'

Mason was a particular friend – a son of Huddersfield whom Brook first met when he was filming *Spring and Port Wine*. He later selected Brook as the only painter in a documentary celebration of his roots, *Home James*, and commissioned him to paint the Mason family home when it was sold.

Tom Courtenay was introduced through a mutual friend. He and Brook hit it off right away. Courtenay has one of Brook's largest paintings, 'Self-portrait Passing a Lamp-post in Birds Royal', in which Brook's already distant figure is half hidden by the post. It was the catalogue cover for his retrospective at the New Grafton Gallery. 'Tom says it's the most modest self-portrait he's ever seen,' he says with a smile.

Another Yorkshire personality who has loomed large in his life – and pictures – is Hannah Hauxwell, whose reclusive and virtually pre-industrial way of living made her a national institution when she was the subject of a TV film. Her farm had no road, no electricity and

He is best loved for his snow scenes, whether of Pennine farms or the road through an empty wood

no water other than what she could carry. She hid in a cow barn when first he called, but soon they were friends and she became the subject of several portraits.

In middle age Brook took up fell-running, Sunday mornings with the Holmfirth Harriers revealing places he says he would otherwise never have found 'because they knew all the obscure passes and that'. He was introduced to the sport by a Cumbrian sheep farmer, Joss Naylor, who owned the holiday cottage the Brooks rented when their daughters, Katharine and Alison, were children. The girls never wanted to go anywhere else so they returned for 15 years and Brook became an adept runner,

taking part in the famous Three Peaks race. Uphill he could hold his own with the champion Joss but 'coming down he'd do it in 17 minutes and I'd take an hour, because he'd let himself go but I couldn't for fear of breaking my arm'.

With Joss he would save 'crag-fast' sheep and sometimes walk the hills at night. 'Keep your dog on the end of a string and follow its white tail – it'll never walk off the edge of a cliff,' he told me. 'It could be quite romantic up there when there were no lights to interfere... The number and distribution of the stars, it made you think how "big" you are.'

The dog was a Border collie. His last, and the most painted, was Shep, who died in June 2004. Shep was selected for him by Jim Cropper, famous breeder and past winner of *One Man and His Dog*. 'Pick one out that looks good to paint, a bright one,' was Brook's request. As can be seen in many of the pictures, Shep had 'lovely chevrons down his back'.

Nowadays agricultural decline means the farms of Brook's youth are derelict, whole valleys often left to be grazed by one farmer's sheep; but the emptiness makes the landscape even more wonderful and 'there's enough interest, with the walls and the colours and the textures and the light, to make a picture.'

Peter Brook has painted the Highlands, Cornwall and, in earlier days, the

All paintings by Peter Brook. Opposite page top: 'The Smell of Wood Smoke'; opposite below: 'The Pennine Landscape' Above: 'A Good View of the Pennines'

mill towns (he still uses the old wooden loom lathes he salvaged to frame his pictures), but he is best loved for his snow scenes, whether of Pennine farms or the road through an empty wood – usually with him and Shep, Everyman and his best friend, lost in the wonder of it all. His explanation is typically unsentimental. 'Things stand out better on a white ground. That's what somebody told Lowry, isn't it? So his pictures are on a white ground whatever the season – you accept it.'

Today he may paint for an hour or so after he has fetched the papers and had a go at the crossword. And he can still have 'good experiences watching snow', even if the milder weather now means it rarely settles for more than a day or two most winters. 'One of the best was watching a road fill up with snow and then a car driving along, leaving its marks, and then the snow coming back and cleaning it away.'

● *For information about original works, prints, publications and forthcoming exhibitions, visit Peter Brook's website at* **www.peterbrookart.co.uk**

Ghost in the machine

GEOFFREY PINK *was invited to attend an interview for a job with a computer company. The following month he was invited to attend again, and again...*

At a time when my job hunt was not going well I was delighted to receive this letter:

> *Wacko Computers Ltd*
> *Wacko House, Windsor Square*
> *London W3*

Dear Mr Pink,

Further to your application to join our Management Training Scheme, please attend for interview in February, bringing with you the enclosed application form, suitably completed.

Your sincerely,
Unreadable signature
Head of Recruitment

'In February' looked wrong, so I telephoned for clarification. After choosing one of five recorded alternatives and one of three options, none of which fitted my question, I finally reached a human. 'Oh,' she said, 'our computer must have had a glitch. It should have said, "attend on 19th February at 9.30".'

I attended. Wacko House was tall,

modern and chromium-plated. There was a gaggle of selectors and two dozen or so candidates, all bright-eyed and bushy-tailed. We were each given a large lapel badge. Mine was Black 4. Others were Blue 2, Red 6 and so on. 'This is to help the selectors during the Group Discussions,' said the Chief Selector. 'You will each also have an interview, an Intelligence Test, a Personality Test and lunch with the Selectors.' It sounded like the

'Going anywhere nice on your sick leave this year, sir?'

Spanish Inquisition on a busy day.

I will not dwell on my performance during this ordeal. The interviewers' questions confused me. The group discussion, a case study of Bill Gates, was over my head. I only completed half the intelligence test in the time allowed and my lunch with the selectors was not noted for sparkling ideas about the future of computing. I was not surprised therefore by:

> *Wacko Computers Ltd*
> *Wacko House, Windsor Square*
> *London W3*

Dear Mr Pink,

We shall not be proceeding with your application, but we would like to thank you for it.

Yours sincerely,
Unreadable signature
Head of Recruitment

That looked like the end of my chances with Wacko Computers. But no. The following week I received:

> *Wacko Computers Ltd*
> *Wacko House, Windsor Square*

London W3

Dear Mr Pink,

Further to your application to join our Management Training Scheme, please attend for interview in March bringing with you the enclosed application form, suitably completed.

Yours sincerely

Unreadable signature

Head of Recruitment

Once again I rang for clarification. Once again, after the inevitable and useless recorded choices and a lot of Vivaldi, I was assured that the computer really meant: 'Come on 19th March at 9.30.' It looked as if the computer was having an attack of repetitive glitch. But then I thought, having nothing to lose, I would 'attend' on 19th March and try my luck again.

My second performance improved beyond recognition. Fortunately they had changed all the interviewers. Mine asked exactly the same questions as his predecessor, and I fielded them with ease. Knowing the intelligence test questions in advance was a big help. They were mostly arithmetical. A calculator and a little homework put me into the genius category. An article in the *Economist* on Bill Gates helped me to shine in the group discussion and did wonders for my lunchtime chat with the selectors. So it was with some surprise that I received another 'No' letter.

I decided that it must have been the personality test that had let me down. However, all was not lost, because within a week came a third invitation. For an unspecified date in April. Same phone call. Same recordings. Same Vivaldi. Different girl. Same answer: 'Come on 19th April at 9.30.'

This time I was determined to win. I bought a book on personality tests, saw where I was going wrong, worked out the right answers, completed the application form for the third time, with embellishments, and set off for the appointment. I was worried about being recognised but, since they seemed to change their selectors each time, this seemed a small risk.

But even small risks happen. 'So,' said the Chief Selector, standing in the doorway, 'you are here again.' I felt that the bottom was about to drop out of my world. But it didn't because he went on: 'Very grateful to you for coming again at such short notice.' Was I in a mad-house? 'Set yourself up in Room 7. The score sheets are there. Same as last time. Black 1 to 6. Forty-five minutes each. Lunch at one. All scores to be in by 3.30. Selectors' meeting at four.'

I found Room 7. On the table were six application forms, marked 'Black 1 to 6'. Then it hit me. He hadn't recognised me. He'd confused me with someone else. He thought I was a selector. One of the application forms was mine – B4. There was a list of candidates' names. I noticed that at 12.15 I would be interviewing me. My attention focused on an envelope marked

There was a list of candidates' names. I noticed that at 12.15 I would be interviewing me

'STRICTLY CONFIDENTIAL'.

I opened it. Inside was a list of the five questions and a score sheet giving the marks for each correct answer. I'd struck oil. The first candidate arrived. Armed with the questions, interviewing the candidates was simple.

At 12.15 I had time to study the scoring system. There were positive marks for certain answers and negative marks for others. I worked out the score for the answers I had given at my last interview. It came out as minus 84. But now I had the key I could score well into the plus 90s, maybe reach plus 100. It was thrilling. Add that to my topmost score in the other tests – heady stuff! Given one more glitch invitation I would break all records. Photo in the House Magazine. Lunch with the Chairman. Glory.

I went to the selectors' meeting at four. There was a huge wall chart showing all the test results of all the candidates. Very impressive. The Chief Selector addressed us. 'I wanted you all to see this before you return to your

various jobs. As you can see, we have removed all questions of bias, opinion and judgment. Human variability and fallibility in the selection process are now things of the past. We shall now input all this data into the computer which will divide the sheep from the goats and write to each candidate accordingly.' There was a murmur of approval. He gazed admiringly at the wall chart. 'Oh,' he said, 'there is no data on candidate Black 4. Why is that?'

'He didn't turn up,' said one of his assistants.

'Damnation! It threatens the whole process when people do things without letting us know. We certainly don't want managers like that in Wacko. Black 4 is a fellow called Pink. I shall override the computer and write to him myself.'

Wacko Computers Ltd
Wacko House, Windsor Square
London W3

Dear Mr Pink,

I have now untangled the thread of your labyrinthine relations with Wacko Computers. I note that your first visit showed that you were not suited for a career in management. Taking unfair advantage of a minor computer error, you proceeded to insinuate yourself into a second visit where, although never mendacious, you presented a thoroughly spurious impression of yourself. Not content with this, you came a third time and passed yourself off as a Selector. Successfully!

Throughout you have shown a brazen ingenuity in exploiting our weaknesses and a remarkable tenacity of purpose. You are clearly not easily put off and I am wondering whether you would consider a career in our sales team. Please let me know.

Yours sincerely,

Unreadable signature

Head of Recruitment

Sex would just ruin what we got

GED

Border skirmishes

Sometimes you really do have to blame the dog…

OBI-WAN KENOBI had little or no time for social norms. Not for him the pedestrian reality of polite obedience and personal boundaries. His was a parallel universe in which he was no mere border terrier but a warrior, a giant, the king of all he surveyed. Cats, dogs, sheep, goats, in fact any mammal with a small mind and a slow turning-circle was fair game to this self-appointed superhero. But he wasn't a superhero. He was, in the words of the local plod, 'a very naughty boy.'

Having waved goodbye to the big city lights in order to give their beloved pet a better life in the countryside, his doting owners, Poshie and Glammie, soon discovered that rural family outings were at best a chore and at worst a legal case waiting to happen.

Desperate to fit in, they had tried everything. Behaviour modification at the very best classes. Treat withdrawal, treat overload, delicate personal surgery that had rendered him useless to even the most persistent of the female sex. They even bought him a friend, a little pup called Kissy Poo, who took one look at her new mate and refused to leave the boot of the car.

Any mammal with a small mind and a slow turning-circle was fair game to this self-appointed superhero

Occasionally, other immigrants would arrive and unwittingly invite them round for drinks. Their rectory doors flung open to make the best of the verdant views, these newcomers were full of the first flush of countryside living and neighbourly bonhomie. 'Bring your dog,' they would say, naively. 'We are very pet-friendly here.'

Invariably, these fledgling relationships didn't last long. Once they had seen what Obi-Wan Kenobi could do to a child's guinea pig, in front of the trauma-tised child, the hosts soon revised their invitation policy. Poshie had lost count of the number of replacement rodents he had bought, but he doubted that anyone else in the village was offered a bulk discount at the local pet store.

Then one day a lunch invitation came from a new couple with no pets and a desire to make friends. Months of social exclusion had taken their toll. Poshie and Glammie were desperate to see the inside of someone else's drinks-cabinet so they decided to risk it.

With nothing worth chasing, Obi-Wan Kenobi was the very picture of good behaviour. 'He's such a good boy,' their hostess commented as the afternoon drew on. 'Perhaps we should get a border terrier.'

Poshie and Glammie were so proud; during one lunch-break he had morphed from an advert for euthanasia to a poster-boy for his breed. The feeling was to be short-lived. While the recently acquainted couples opened their third bottle of Chardonnay, Obi-Wan Kenobi decided to take a look inside the garage.

The triumphant howls could only mean one thing. 'Ooh,' said Glammie, trying to cover her alarm at the all too familiar sound. 'What could that be?' Paolo, the eighty-year-old South American tortoise, had never met a dog before, and from his compromised position, he wasn't keen to repeat the experience.

'Paolo,' sobbed his distraught owners. 'Paolo, Paolo.' Paolo was busy trying to keep breathing while Obi-Wan Kenobi helpfully swung him round by his leg. The specialist vet arrived and said it might be touch and go and would certainly be expensive. With no alternative, Poshie immediately offered to pay all the bills as they retrieved the mortified reptile from the jaws of his assailant.

After several days on 24-hour observation, it appeared that there was no immediate threat to Paolo's life except perhaps Poshie's desire to bring an end to the mounting invoices. Unfortunately for him, the vet was in no rush. Apparently tortoises are as slow to mend as they are to move. It could be 2018 before he is discharged. 'It's the worse case of "tortoise interruptus" I've ever seen,' he added. 'I wouldn't bank on it,' replied Poshie.

More from
the Whiteboard
jungle

Drunk, bawdy – and that's just the teachers. Kate Sawyer on the Year 11 prom

Exams are followed by the joy of the Year 11s leaving, and then their 'prom'. This is a curiously American phenomenon that has, like so much else American, been taken up here. Hamburgers, war and proms – where they lead, we follow.

The prom is a celebration of having achieved five years at secondary school, of having sat ten GCSEs, of being young and hopeful and on the brink of life. It is also an excellent carrot/stick to hold up to the increasingly disaffected 16-year-olds as they lurch towards the final post. The children (well, the girls) start planning what they will wear and who will partner them in Year 7. By Year 11, when they should be concentrating on John Steinbeck and limestone, they are saving up for their dresses, their 'makeovers' (piles of dyed hair and thick layers of unnecessary make up) and – most importantly – how they will make their entrances. So, it is at that vital time that the bribery/threats really kick in. The greatest punishment in the entire secondary school system is being banned from the prom. It is meant to make the children work, behave well, and, above all, not turn up drunk on the last day of school. It's a pity we can only use it once.

There is something wonderful in the students' arrival at their dance, held at a local country club. They come in milk floats, fire engines, army vehicles and, of course, a fleet of pink Playboy limos. Only the very socially secure jocks (see how naturally American vocabulary creeps in) dare to walk up the drive on their own two feet. Others come in everything from helicopters (£200 a time) to 'borrowed' supermarket trolleys decorated with balloons. Parents line up to see their children arrive, with tiny siblings dressed in their own versions of ball gowns.

The teachers dress up too and it's important to do this right. Over-dress, and you're stealing the students' thunder; under-dress and you're not showing them 'respect'. Teachers' responsibility does

> *They come in milk floats, fire engines, army vehicles and, of course, a fleet of pink limos*

not end there, and this is where it can go horrifically wrong. To encourage us to go, we are invited free and given wine at our table. And how embarrassing we can be. PE teachers are the worst, perhaps because they are often the youngest. One flashed her bosom, told a boy how attractive he was and was then sick. Others fought over the karaoke, pushing children aside, shouting 'It's my turn' and warbling Abba badly.

Meanwhile the children – many of whom have never sat down to a three-course meal before – are overawed by the glamour of the country club and the boys in dinner jackets. I once spent half an hour with a sobbing girl who said that she could not walk through a room full of people wearing a dress. She couldn't: she hauled up her dress and fell off her shoes. I ran her through the whole fake confidence thing – chin up, stomach in, sashay, sashay, smile – until I made her laugh, and sent her out of the loos ahead of me with her shoulders back. I was probably more useful to her then than in Year 8 when I taught her about metaphors and etymology.

If you try to book a computer room you are usually blocked by the cooking department. Which strikes me as odd. I was taught to cook two dishes at school – mash (Smash) with cheese on top and drumsticks with Campbell's condensed mushroom soup. Neither was cooking as I know it. But at least it involved a pan of some kind. Now it's all to do with knowing what a carb is and how to wash a can of tomatoes before you open it. One class was told to stand around and watch the 'best ever custard' being made – and was then given a masterclass on how to whisk Bird's custard powder.

The government has now announced, that cooking is to move from 'designing' to 'making'. So instead of designing a sandwich they will make one. When these children have a family I hope they'll be able to make a sandwich in less than an hour. Forget Dickens – that will prove that the education system is successful.

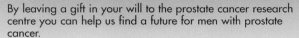

'If this were a resort hotel, you couldn't afford to stay here,' I tell prisoner number 490277. (Not his real number: integers have been changed to protect the convicted.) He smiles and sits in the grey chair. Visitors use red ones.

Wife and I are visiting a British friend serving a life sentence in a Southern state. The institution's setting is idyllic, in a verdant hollow ringed by mountains, so the 20-foot-high razor wire is more grotesque, like a tank in Avalon.

We sit with 20 or so other groups in the 'visitation' room, asking questions we've rehearsed on the way here. How is your carpentry class? Is the radio reception good? Any word on a possible repatriation? Bill (another alias) points out a heavyset, bearded man across the room, whom I'd pegged as a biker doing time for GBH. 'Not at all,' he says. 'Great pal of mine. Works in the library. He's in here for the same, er, problem that I had.'

Bill's 'problem' was killing his wife, who'd been unfaithful.

Incongruously, there's a huge *trompe l'oeil* mural behind us depicting the seasons. 'Old Jasper did that,' Bill explains. 'He was even more obsessed with time than most of us. Gone now,' he adds, leaving us to speculate on what 'gone' means.

It's very warm, and he swivels to ask a guard if he can roll up the sleeves of his grey nylon shirt. Wife and I both check the shirt for numbers, but there are none.

'It's so great to see you,' Bill says for the third time. Apart from a court-appointed attorney and a brief interview with someone from the British Consulate, he has received no visitors since being sentenced five years ago.

'If I'd committed my crime in England, I'd have got about seven years, and maybe served five,' he says with some bitterness. 'I'm not trying to excuse what I did, but surely life was too much under the circumstances?'

Much too much, we agree. Heck, even the doctor who'd prescribed the Prozac Bill was taking at the time wrote him an apology. 'But wasn't that brought up at the trial?' I ask.

'They didn't seem to think it was relevant.'

Until two years ago, he had edited the prison newsletter, coaxing essays and letters and artwork from even the most laconic. But the co-ordinator of this programme had been laid off as a result of budgetary constraints, so now the computer gathered dust in a locked room.

Killing time

NICK HOBART *and his wife went to see a friend serving a life term in jail in a Southern American state – his first visitors since he was sentenced five years ago*

Bill's 'problem' was killing his wife, who'd been un-faithful – 'In England I'd have got about seven years'

'Really enjoyed doing that,' Bill says wistfully. 'And none of the other staff...?' I let the question die, seeing his slow headshake.

Wife's eyes have been flicking around the tables, and she says, 'I'm rather surprised there aren't more, er, you know...'

'Blacks? It's about 50–50 here, but only a few of them ever get visitors.'

'Would many of them be from out of state?' After all, we've come from Florida.

'A few, but mostly the family either doesn't care or can't afford to get here. It is a bit isolated.'

Time's nearly up, and the guards are conferring, planning their eviction strategy.

'If they repatriated you, wouldn't the British authorities have the power to shorten your sentence?'

'That seems to be moot,' he replies instantly, clearly having thought about it. 'They try to co-operate with the state guidelines, but...'

'And would you have any kind of say about location?' Even as I ask the question, it sounds naïve.

'No. You go to some processing centre – Wormwood Scrubs, probably – and then you're assigned...'

There has been no whistle or bell, but mothers and wives and girlfriends are hugging, and blue uniforms herd us towards the metal door while the residents remain seated.

'Stiff upper lip,' I say, and instantly feel foolish. 'I'll write as soon as we get back.'

Bill's smiling as the door clangs shut behind us. Outside in the bright sun the dogwoods are in blossom, and a paraphrase of Henry Reed's 'Naming of Parts' comes to mind. 'This is the Spring, and this is Liberty, which in your case you have not got.'

Now I am nearly eighty

PHILIP CALLOW *spent his younger days worrying about his life and career. In old age, he has discovered, you can indulge in the most useless occupations without guilt*

I can't believe – isn't it the same for all of us? – that very soon I shall be 79, entering my 80th year. How could it have happened? Why wasn't I paying attention, allowing all those years to slip away so slyly? Like the jazz player aged 100, I feel like joking that if I'd known I was going to live this long I would have taken better care of myself. Now that it is a fact, I am in the position of so many others, looking back at my life and wondering if I could have lived it differently. But did I have a choice?

From the very beginning I found myself with a job that I disliked, one that worried me to death with its precision, a job stretching ahead for years without a break. I was an apprentice toolmaker, indentured for six years because my father thought it would be good for me to have a trade, something he regretted not having himself as a clerk, after surviving the Depression by the skin of his teeth. In those days you did your best to oblige your father, and in any case I had no idea what I wanted to do. My father proudly signed his name on the apprenticeship papers and my fate was sealed.

It occurs to me now that I turned to serious reading and then writing during those worrying years when I was living a lie, learning to be a toolmaker and pretending to like it. One day I was sure I would be found out and exposed, seen to be a failure. When I tried imitating the short stories and poems I was reading I became absorbed in something just as intricate as the hated toolmaking but somehow altogether more satisfying, fitting sentences together and making them flow like the cutting oil of the machines I had to operate. This new skill did not give me oil-dermatitis, and best of all there was no boss, only myself to satisfy.

Although I was beginning to cultivate a knack for words that would be an even longer apprenticeship, this only applied to the written word. Face to face with a girl, for instance, I was as tongue-tied as any other painfully self-conscious apprentice. Teenagers who were full of confidence were uncommon in those days, and there was no money and nowhere to go.

Born of a worried mother and a potentially gregarious, shy father, a gentle soul disguised as an iron man, I remember one morning an extraordinary booming, priestly voice on the radio when I was a child. This was Dylan Thomas, reading the majestic lines of Milton's Satan. I didn't of course know how funny he

> ### There is endless time to please yourself, the moment you abolish the need to accomplish something

would have thought that, this clown-poet who spilled desperate jokes and wrote terrible begging letters, a thief who would steal a shirt and leave his own dirty one under his host's bed. I only thought how beautiful to make a sound like that, to be a poet in this town, Coventry, and in this household, that knew all about carburettors and nothing about poetry.

I recognise in myself my mother's fears, and for a long time have glimpsed my father in the mirror. But this is not meant to be about me. It is about my own and others' years, that fall from us like leaves and bring us to autumn and then winter.

To be nearly eighty is to run out of choices, to stop asking the way. I thought at first that I wanted to be a painter, but was afraid of failure. 'Not every picture has to be a masterpiece,' said Picasso. George Orwell saw his life as a whole series of failures, convinced that failure was more honourable than success. The truth is that the very idea of failure loses its meaning when you are approaching eighty. Time rushes along, faster than ever, and yet there is endless time to please yourself, the moment you abolish the need to accomplish something. If you have not achieved your ambition, whatever it is, there is no point in starting now. The burdens fall away, and you can spend time on the most useless occupations without guilt, such as watching the big black insouciant cat from next door as it saunters up the path. You are happy to see it, to welcome it, and at the same time you are concerned for the young robin that has just alighted on your bird table and is fixing bright new eyes on you with that astonishing intimacy robins have.

In other words, you are shedding what is left of your ego and coming close to the one sure joy you can be certain of in old age. You are close to forgetting about yourself. Who knows, you might soon be free of yourself entirely one fine day.

I love older men... they're not trying to impress you all the time

GED